Media and Moral Education

Media and Moral Education demonstrates that the study of philosophy can be used to enhance critical thinking skills, which are sorely needed in today's technological age. It addresses the current oversight of the educational environment not keeping pace with rapid advances in technology, despite the fact that educating students to engage critically and compassionately with others via online media is of the utmost importance.

D'Olimpio claims that philosophical thinking skills support the adoption of an attitude she calls critical perspectivism, which she applies in the book to international multimedia examples. The author also suggests that the Community of Inquiry – a pedagogy practised by advocates of Philosophy for Children – creates a space in which participants can practise being critically perspectival, and can be conducted with all age levels in a classroom or public setting, making it beneficial in shaping democratic and discerning citizens.

This book will be of interest to academics, researchers and postgraduate students in the areas of philosophy of education, philosophy, education, critical theory and communication, film and media studies.

Dr Laura D'Olimpio is a Senior Lecturer in Philosophy at the University of Notre Dame Australia.

Routledge International Studies in the Philosophy of Education

For more titles in the series, please visit www.routledge.com/Routledge-International-Studies-in-the-Philosophy-of-Education/book-series/SE0237

Media and Moral Education
A Philosophy of Critical Engagement
Laura D'Olimpio

Philosophy, Dialogue, and Education
Nine Modern European Philosophers
Alexandre Guilherme and W. John Morgan

Heidegger During the Turn
Poetry, Literature, and Education
James M. Magrini and Elias Schwieler

In Community of Inquiry with Ann Margaret Sharp
Childhood, Philosophy and Education
Edited by Megan Jane Laverty and Maughn Rollins Gregory

Technologies of Being in Martin Heidegger
Nearness, Metaphor and the Question of Education in Digital Times
Anna Kouppanou

Creating the Practical Man of Modernity
The Reception of John Dewey's Pedagogy in Mexico
Victor J. Rodriguez

Reinventing Intercultural Education
A Metaphysical Manifest for Rethinking Cultural Diversity
Neal Dreamson

Teachability and Learnability
Can Thinking Be Taught?
Paul Fairfield

Neuroscience and Education
A Philosophical Appraisal
Edited by Clarence W. Joldersma

Media and Moral Education
A Philosophy of Critical Engagement

Laura D'Olimpio

Routledge
Taylor & Francis Group

LONDON AND NEW YORK

First published 2018
by Routledge
2 Park Square, Milton Park, Abingdon, Oxon OX14 4RN

and by Routledge
711 Third Avenue, New York, NY 10017

Routledge is an imprint of the Taylor & Francis Group, an informa business

© 2018 Laura D'Olimpio

British Library Cataloguing-in-Publication Data
A catalogue record for this book is available from the British Library

Library of Congress Cataloging-in-Publication Data
A catalog record for this book has been requested

ISBN: 978-1-138-29142-3 (hbk)
ISBN: 978-1-315-26545-2 (ebk)

Typeset in Galliard
by Apex CoVantage, LLC

Printed and bound by CPI Group (UK) Ltd, Croydon, CR0 4YY

For all the teachers, past, present, and future.

Contents

Acknowledgements

I am grateful to my family, friends, students and colleagues for their encouragement and support of my work on this book. In particular I would like to thank Michael Hand, Andrew Peterson, Michael Levine and Christoph Teschers for reading and providing feedback on draft versions of my proposal and chapters and for spotting my occasionally hilarious typos. Without these exchanges with friends and mentors, the ideas in this book would surely have been expressed in a less refined manner. I am also grateful to my peers within the philosophy for children and philosophy of education communities. Your enthusiasm for teaching young people critical thinking skills and the role philosophy has to play in improving society constantly inspires me and makes me happy to be working in this area. Conversations with my peers within the Association for Philosophy in Schools (APIS, WA), the Federation of Australasian Philosophy in Schools Associations (FAPSA) and the Philosophy of Education Society of Australasia (PESA), as well as attendance at their conferences and workshops, have all been rewarding and a good testing ground for my ideas in their various stages of development. Thanks to the University of Notre Dame Australia, which has helped fund my attendance at these conferences. Thanks also to Routledge for their editorial support. Last but not least, thank you to my husband for his loving support and many cups of tea.

Introduction

Critical thinking skills are sorely needed in contemporary society, with its focus on knowledge, technology and connectedness. As global citizens, we receive more information and images than ever previously, thanks to our technological devices, the Internet and the plethora of online sharing platforms. When it comes to mass art and social media, we need to discern between reliable sources of information, misinformation, hoaxes, scams and fake news. The discerning citizen will be able to engage critically, creatively, collaboratively and compassionately with multiple sources and diverse perspectives encountered on a daily basis.

In our contemporary world, teaching people to engage critically and compassionately with others via online media is of vital importance. Educational environments such as schools have struggled to keep up with rapid advancements in technology. Moral agents use rational emotions such as compassion to imagine 'what it is like' for others prior to deciding how they should act. Social media allows us to engage imaginatively with stories of diverse others globally. Teaching transferable skills such as critical thinking and moral engagement through the study of philosophy is one way that moral education may occur, allowing students to apply these skills online.

It is important that we educate people to be able to think for themselves. Adopting a democratic and inclusive attitude, a discerning citizen will encourage conversations that seek to dispel ignorance, recognising pluralism but rejecting relativism. Relativists believe that the truth, or moral truth, is completely subjective and relative either to the individual (known as subjectivism) or to a cultural group (cultural relativism). The problem with this position is that it does not allow for shared moral values or objective truth and it implies that all opinions are of equal value (whether that refers to truth or moral value). However, even where there are individual and cultural differences, there are also shared human values and discoverable truths we are justified in believing. In seeking to be ethically engaged, the moral agent will critically and compassionately investigate claims and assumptions, stereotypes and values conveyed by multimedia sources. As such sources are commonplace, we should embrace them and engage with them appropriately. For these reasons and more, it will also become obvious that philosophers have an important role to play within both educative settings and public spaces.

In this book, I have two main aims. Firstly, to detail and defend a particular moral attitude that should be adopted when engaging with multiple sources of information, particularly information received via technological media. I call this attitude 'critical perspectivism'. Critical perspectivism gives us the ability to engage with multiple perspectives in a critical, yet compassionate, manner. This approach is holistic and pragmatic in that it assumes that people are rational as well as affective creatures, situated in a context. In order to be engaged in a critically perspectival manner, one must be educated to be critical, compassionate and collaborative in one's approach to learning, receiving and transmitting information. My second main aim is to explain how we may teach people to be critically perspectival and encourage them to adopt this attitude. After introducing the concept and explaining why I believe that critical perspectivism is necessary in today's global, technological world, I will argue that this mode of attention can be modelled, taught and practised in order to form a habit. Such practise may take place within a classroom setting, or in a forum where public philosophy is being offered, for instance in a philosophy café that employs a method of Socratic dialogue. These examples will be fleshed out further in the book, but it will become apparent that critical perspectivism sees philosophy as a praxis, and the work of the philosopher as educator or public intellectual can complement and supplement the valuable work of philosophy in the academy.

In order to illustrate my second main claim, I will show how critical perspectivism may be cultivated by the philosophy in schools or philosophy for children (P4C) pedagogy, which includes the community of inquiry (CoI) methodology. In an educational context, there is an increasing awareness of the need to prepare students not simply for exams but also for life. When it comes to educational institutions, which specialise in the production of knowledge, we should include the study of philosophy into the curriculum. Philosophy teaches critical thinking skills that are required for children to become informed, socially situated learners (Millett & Tapper, 2012; Golding, Gurr & Hinton, 2012; Burgh, Field & Freakley, 2006; Lipman, 2003; Splitter & Sharp, 1995). I will focus on the knower who possesses the intellectual virtue of discernment and claim that the CoI method as practised by proponents of P4C is a useful tool by which to develop and encourage critical, caring, creative and collaborative thinking skills that can be applied to engagement with everyday moral dilemmas, mass art and social media.

When referring to social media, the definition given by Boyd and Ellison (2008, p. 211) will prove useful:

> We define social network sites as web-based services that allow individuals to (1) construct a public or semi-public profile within a bounded system, (2) articulate a list of other users with whom they share a connection, and (3) view and traverse their list of connections and those made by others within the system.

So why is this so important? Why do we need to teach people how to engage respectfully but also critically with online information and virtual others?

Technological advancements have ushered in an age whereby the way social media and the Internet are used has changed our lives, including the way we seek out information, the way we spend our leisure time and how we communicate with one another. The vast majority (92%) of American teenagers use social media daily, aided by the widespread availability of smart phones (Lenhart, 2015). In Australia, 79% of people access the Internet daily and 68% of Internet users have a social media profile, with the majority of them (70%) accessing social media via a smartphone and using an application (app) (Sensis, 2015). Significantly, most of these young people learn how to use technology and social network sites informally, through their engagement with such sites and from their peers, rather than from their parents or teachers.

Young people today are referred to as digital natives, meaning that they have only ever known a time when the Internet existed and they have grown up with this technology. The advent of Web 2.0 (replacing the WWW or World Wide Web, which is retrospectively called Web 1.0) was heralded as liberating and is characterised by increased participation as pervasive network connectivity and communication channels encourage greater use and collaboration. However, although young people are growing up with the Internet, this does not mean they are born with skills to use it in a savvy and safe or even respectful manner. Such skills, or multiliteracies as I refer to them, must still be learned. Today's Web 2.0 allows for the democratisation of the Internet, as users include individuals as well as groups, institutions, companies and governments. Such accessibility has supported and, in turn, been supported by neoliberal policies which advocate corporate deregulation, privatisation, competition, entrepreneurialism and open markets to achieve both financial success and individual self-actualisation. "While these policies have met with global protests, they have become the predominant paradigm of the twenty-first century" (Marwick, 2013, p. 11).

In this brave new world, famous personalities can reveal immediate and intimate insights into their lives, companies can advertise directly to their market consumer base and expand their brand globally in a short space of time, clients and customers have immediate access to space to voice their praise or frustration at products, services, and their voices are heard and may be responded to immediately. The number of voices are staggering. Users (of all kinds and affiliations) have the chance to alter and impact upon the Internet and its information contained therein, which is updated and changed in real time. The social nature of Web 2.0 differentiates it from the static WWW that went before. Web 2.0 also allows social media companies to have a lot of power and even more profit (Marwick, 2013, p. 4) as they use, and often struggle to keep up with, social platforms that include wikis, social networking, social bookmarking, forums, blogs, applications and interactive websites.

Meanwhile, it is the technology industry that benefits financially, as consumers laud the products produced at a rapid rate. In the US, this industry has remained profitable in an otherwise difficult economy with venture capital funding in San Francisco, 'the centre of the social media world' and home of Google, Facebook and Twitter, increasing between 2007–2011 despite the economic downturn (Marwick, 2013, pp. 3–4). The profitability of the technology industry and the desire of consumers for new gadgets show no signs of abating. In tension with the enthusiasm for what new technology can do for us is a worry about what such technology is doing *to* us. Researchers worry about increased levels of narcissism, anxiety about online bullying, decreased attention spans, antisocial behaviour including the recruitment of vulnerable youths to extremist military organisations, cyber terrorism and the propagation of misinformation, hoaxes and scams.

We must ask whether or not such fears are well founded or if these risks are any higher than they have previously been. The risks present in today's technological society may take a different form and are able to manifest in a new way due to the technology available, but this alone does not prove that we should be more alert and alarmed than usual. However, it does mean that we need to consider the best way to engage online with others and with the information we receive. A particular focus of moral concern is on the young and what can be done to protect them online.

It is important to point out that the online world is just as real as the ordinary world. This is not a make-believe world such as that you may encounter in a fictional narrative. There may be virtual and fictional aspects to the online world, such as avatars through which one portrays oneself, and our ability to do certain things is different in virtual space. Obviously one's embodiment alters as the body we use online is decontextualised and nonphysical. Yet there are real others with whom one interacts, whether they be people users know in real life and have met face-to-face or not. Ultimately, it will be critical thinking skills such as rational discernment and the moral attitude of compassion that is contextually applied that will best serve users, young and not-so-young, of social media. Pragmatically, such transferable thinking skills serve us well in life, and these skills may be applied online. A good way of educating such critical thinking skills and moral dispositions is through the study of philosophy, particularly through methodologies used by P4C practitioners. Thus, the study of philosophy may prove useful in assisting students to learn how to effectively engage with technologically mediated sources of information that are ubiquitous in the twenty-first century.

Critical perspectivism

My first chapter will be dedicated to detailing critical perspectivism, a moral attitude that may be practised and adopted when engaging with multiple sources of information. It is an attitude that supports a practise of being morally engaged in the world by processing and understanding information received from mass-produced and distributed media sources in a critical and compassionate manner. Much of the information (including images) we encounter contains implicit or explicit social, political and moral messages that need to be approached actively and critically with a caring response to real-life others. As technology increases the rate and amount of information we receive, we must seek to morally evaluate and assimilate useful information, while discarding misinformation, and avoiding hoaxes and scams.

Critical perspectivism has two central features: it is compassionate and it is critical. In chapters two and three, I will examine each of these features in turn, considering the role they play in our responses to people and mediated information, with the aim of seeking knowledge, wisdom and ethical relationships.

Compassion

Chapter two focusses on how ethical agents engage in a compassionate and imaginative manner with others, drawing upon the moral philosophy of contemporary virtue ethicist Martha Nussbaum. Nussbaum explores and defends the rational emotion of compassion as a moral or 'loving' attitude. She claims that this loving attitude may be practised in response to narrative artworks, which may assist in the moral education of readers. Thus, Nussbaum (1987) claims that moral philosophy would be improved by the addition of aesthetically and ethically good narrative artworks that provide readers with the opportunity to practise ethical decision-making skills. Adopting a framework of virtue ethics, Nussbaum makes a teleological claim that good art aids moral education. People who engage with such works have the opportunity to practise their ethical responses to life-like situations depicted in works of fiction. Such practise encourages the use of their moral imagination in a positive manner in everyday life.

In her later writings, Nussbaum (1995, p. 6) extends her theory to include film as an example of narrative art. If Nussbaum is correct, the potential exists for mass artworks, such as films, to be used to illuminate moral dilemmas for the viewer, as narrative artworks allow for the realistic and nuanced portrayal of life. It may be that we can learn from the diverse perspectives offered to us via mass art and social media, although the technological features of such media will have to be carefully considered and critiqued. I will critically investigate Nussbaum's notion of an ethical mode of attention and consider whether this argument could be extended to mass art and social media. My main focus is on whether Nussbaum's loving and compassionate attitude as a moral attitude to be adopted towards others is adequate for those engaging with mass information and multimedia sources.

I am sympathetic to the idea that, by practicing what Nussbaum calls a 'loving attitude', her version of ethical attention, we can form virtuous habits that lead to *phronesis* (practical wisdom). However, my worry is that if we over-emphasise the affective component of compassion, we may forget to be critical and apply the appropriate amount of distance between ourselves and those who suffer, thereby rendering our ethical engagement with them biased and emotive rather than rational. In an Aristotelian sense, we must find the golden mean for our actions to be considered virtuous. Furthermore, in our contemporary, technological society with multiple perspectives constantly bombarding us, there is a need to maintain a healthy dose of critical distance and scepticism even while remaining compassionate to the suffering of real-life others. Thus, I defend critical perspectivism as an enhanced moral attitude that encourages moral agents to critically evaluate information and figure out the appropriately rational and compassionate response to people and situations, while seeking appropriate evidence for their beliefs.

The moral possibilities of mass art and media

After granting that compassion is an important part of a moral attitude one should adopt when seeking to make ethical decisions, chapter three further explores why a moral agent must be critical and cautious when negotiating technologically mediated sources of information. To this end, chapter three sets the scene by engaging with the approaches taken towards mass art within the field of philosophical aesthetics. Historically, philosophers in the Anglo-American, typically analytic, tradition have been very resistant to including mass-produced and distributed artworks into the category of art *qua* Art proper. Theorists such as R. G. Collingwood (1938), Dwight MacDonald (1963), Clement Greenberg (1971), T. W. Adorno and Max Horkheimer (1997) have worried that mass art is pseudo art and encourages passive spectatorship. The interesting aspect to this seemingly elitist critique is the moral concern that appears to underlie their theories. By excluding, for example, film from the category of art due to its technical means of production (and reproduction), these theorists demonise the medium and mistakenly consider all mass art to be *bad*, both ethically as well as aesthetically.

Times have changed, and many contemporary philosophers now embrace mass art and film as art and as vehicles for the portrayal and exploration of philosophical ideas. Theorists such as Walter Benjamin (1969), Gilles Deleuze (1986; 1989), Thomas Wartenberg (2007), Stephen Mulhall (2002) and Daniel Frampton (2006) embrace 'filmosophy' and celebrate, in particular, the work of film auteurs. This positive reaction to film sees mass art as able to abet active and critically engaged spectatorship, and includes the possibility of philosophical learning via watching and engaging with (certain) films. When it comes to films, I claim that we need to consider what the masses are watching alongside what can be achieved with mass art and, as such, I argue for a moderate approach to mass art (D'Olimpio, 2014). This moderate approach entails taking seriously the ethical concerns of those traditional theorists who were pessimistic about the effects of mass art and also embraces the optimistic perspective that mass art may encourage critical spectatorship and transmit philosophical ideas in an exciting manner to large audiences.

The reason I adopt this moderate approach is because I am interested in the educative potential of technologically produced and distributed works. The focus of our discussion should be on the critical thinker who is receiving, engaging with and possibly transmitting the work and/or its message to others. This is where the attitude of critical perspectivism is of vital importance. In considering how spectators read such stories, we can extend this critique to other social media forms and consider how users of social media may also be able to engage critically and empathetically with one another and with the stories of diverse others.

In our global, technologically connected world, the key skill of multiliteracies (Cope & Kalantzis, 2000) is gaining prominence. As technology changes so quickly, I believe the sensible thing to do is to educate citizens to be critical, compassionate and collaborative as well as creative in their approach to what they see and hear. This way, even as the mediums alter in ways we could not hope to foresee or imagine, people will be able to ask not just 'what', 'how' and 'where' but also 'why'. The 'why' questions are of paramount importance, as they include moral questions such as 'should we . . .'? Thus, chapter three details the approach to mass art that has changed over time, as technology becomes increasingly a part of our everyday lives and takes seriously the ethical as well as the aesthetic concerns of philosophers who recognise the power of social media, images, film and television in society.

Any account of the role mass art may play in society must take into account the concerns theorists such as Adorno and Horkheimer (1997) outline with regard to the dominance of mass cultural works that promote a passive audience response. One reason mass art succumbs to aesthetic and ethical criticism has to do with its production and consumption within a market of monopoly capitalism. Moral dilemmas associated with mass cultural products that aim to achieve economic as opposed to aesthetic ends, although not inherent in the medium or production methods itself, are a factor of which consumers and artists should be aware. Pro-mass art theorists such as Walter Benjamin (1969) need to consider how mass artworks may combat the promotion of a non-reflective, passive audience response that encourages viewers to 'switch off' their critical voice.

Much like my approach to the narrative artworks used as examples in chapter two, I do not see any point in labelling all artworks of a certain form 'good' or 'bad' based solely on their uniqueness or accessibility, their mass production or consumption, or their formal features, even where such features may incline artworks and mass-produced and distributed products to be better or worse (aesthetically and/or ethically). My focus remains on the attitude of the viewer engaging with and receiving such works along with the messages contained therein. While I argue that artists and technicians and users of technology also have an ethical obligation to create and use such works and media in ethical ways, I am focussed on the ethical attitude of critical perspectivism that may be taught, exemplified and practised. Critical perspectivism is a moral attitude that may be applied to multiple sources of information and media that we encounter every day. In this way it is holistic and pragmatic and demands that moral agents be critically as well as compassionately engaged with the world.

Multiliteracies

Chapter four focusses on some examples that highlight why it is so important to teach people to adopt an attitude of critical perspectivism. Using three examples of the perils and pitfalls of social media; namely, hoaxes, scams and catfishing, I defend the sentiment echoed by those theorists who speak about multiliteracies. Specifically, "students must be agents of text rather than victims of text, whether that text is printed and found in school or visually digitized and found in the street" (Albers & Hartse, 2007, p. 7). Society needs critical thinkers who are also engaged morally as citizens, people who are compassionate as well as practical.

It is a unique feature of the contemporary world that we have access to more information and images, opinions and various perspectives than ever previously thanks to our global technology and connectivity. As every individual may broadcast their ideas and experiences to everyone else instantaneously, and statements may be fact checked against the truth using evidence, statistics, corroboration etcetera, it seems strangely perverse that the Oxford Dictionary's 2016 word of the year is 'post-truth': an adjective defined as 'relating to or denoting circumstances in which objective facts are less influential in shaping public opinion than appeals to emotion and personal belief.'

The post-truth climate that has now been identified seems to be supported by the proliferation of multiple perspectives available to anyone with Internet access. As users may log on and find a statement, website, or misquote that supports anything they already believe or something they wish or fear to be true, and are able to chat with others with whom they agree, an echo-chamber is set up that reinforces the idea, regardless of its veracity. Further, arguments with others with whom they disagree do not seem to dispel the ignorance, unlike what is aimed for in a Socratic dialogue. Rather, such debate may reinforce the biased or blatantly false view through what behavioural psychologists term the 'familiarity backfire effect' (Cook & Lewandowsky, 2011). The backfire effect may be seen in relation to the attempt to debunk false views, such as when responding to climate change deniers or anti-vaccination supporters. By mentioning 'climate change science', or by fact checking claims of anti-vaxxers, such attempts serve only to reinforce the myths, with Cook and Lewandowsky noting that "a simple myth is more cognitively attractive than an over-complicated correction" (2011, p. 3). Such worrying attitudes towards truth and evidence epitomise how popularity, sensationalism and 'reassuring' myths (it is more reassuring to think that climate change is false) and false beliefs hold much sway and political power in the world today.

This problem of subjectivism is particularly evident online as, with our technological capabilities, we have access to many various ideas through blogs, news websites of varying journalistic quality, satirical websites, self-created and uploaded videos, images and memes, discussion boards and chat applications, not to mention advertisements and predatory messages, all with varying levels of privacy. We seek out information and we stumble across it, and we want people to be able to understand and process what they find. In learning to distinguish between valuable sources of reliable information and the plethora of dross, I argue that the best answer lies not in censorship necessarily, but, rather, in teaching those who engage with such mediums the ability to critically discern between them.

Within the field of educational pedagogy, there is a discussion about the need to educate students in what may be called multiliteracies (Kalantzis & Cope, 2012) as the need for educational institutions to catch up and keep up with the speed of individual technological literacy is felt. Children today are learning more about literacy outside of school than they are in, especially through electronic and digital devices and software. Teachers increasingly need to look critically at the influence of media on in-school and out-of-school literacies, and educational institutions cannot afford to ignore these new media platforms. Technological tools must be embraced if we wish to teach students to engage with them critically as well as creatively. Literacy is reinventing itself, with the advent of new information technologies and the complex multiliteracies allowed by them; but the critical thinking skills required to engage with different texts is the same. After considering some examples of why critical perspectivism is needed for online engagement, chapter five examines how we might teach people to be critically perspectival.

Education

Chapter five highlights the need to cultivate in children and adults a habit of engaging critically with what they see and hear. Critical perspectivism is necessary in today's world because it gives us the ability to engage with multiple perspectives and still judge: to be critical, caring and compassionate while recognising the context in which dialogue and interactions take place. There are some assumptions embedded in my defence of critical perspectivism, including the fact that human beings are logical/rational *and* emotional. In a practical, holistic approach, we must focus not only on developing critical thinking skills, but also on appropriately employing and acting upon rational emotions such as compassion. It is the combination of being critical as well as caring that supports a critically perspectival approach to knowledge and to others with whom we interact online or face-to-face. I defend the use of philosophy as a praxis to habituate critical, caring, creative and collaborative citizens who are democratic but also still make normative judgements with respect to what is good. In order to illustrate my arguments, I draw upon P4C and the CoI pedagogy.

Matthew Lipman (2003) started P4C together with Ann Sharp in the 1970s in America, drawing upon the pragmatic philosophy of John Dewey (1997; 2008). Claiming that philosophy need not be confined to universities, Lipman maintained that children could practise critical thinking skills through the use of dialogue and by using specifically written, age-appropriate philosophical narratives as a stimulus text. Lipman defines critical thinking as "thinking that (1) facilitates judgment because it (2) relies on criteria, (3) is self-correcting, and (4) is sensitive to context" (2003, p. 212). By thoughtfully discussing stories that contain philosophical concepts, Lipman hoped to encourage children to ultimately develop into reasonable and democratic citizens. Along with critical thinking skills, Laurance J. Splitter and Ann Sharp (1995) added 'caring' and 'creative' thinking as equally important skills children should be encouraged to develop. Therefore, P4C aims at shaping critical, caring and creative thinkers who are able to work collaboratively as members of a group in search of truth.

One way in which teachers facilitate P4C in their classroom is through a CoI whereby participants sit in an inward-facing circle to engage in a dialogue based on a particular topic, usually seeking to explore a stimulus question that is open and philosophical (Cam, 2006). In order to generate the students' questions, teachers may firstly read a text such as *Thinking Stories* (Cam, 1993) and facilitate an activity using a Question Quadrant (Cam, 2006). The questions children come up with can be scribed by the teacher on a whiteboard and then voted upon in order to gain a consensus as to which question should be the central focus of the CoI. The CoI is guided by the line of inquiry that develops, and the teacher is a facilitator rather than the one source of 'correct' answers. This radicalises the role of teacher as a member of a community that is thinking alongside children as opposed to simply giving students information that they need to learn and be able to recite (Kennedy, 2015). The CoI takes seriously the idea that children have their own ideas, questions and voices that are worth voicing, listening to and exploring. This challenges the perceived gap between adults and children, creating a space whereby adults can listen carefully for children's wisdom (Vansieleghem & Kennedy, 2012, p. 5).

The aim of the CoI is to encourage children to think for themselves and to learn to trust their own capacity for rationality and prudence. Thinking is thus individual and collective: there is the reflective thinking that is done as an isolated individual and there is also the thinking that is done in a group whereby ideas are built upon communally as well as challenged or questioned. The CoI may assist participants to explore ideas collaboratively and thus grow in self-esteem and confidence as they recognise themselves as one amongst a group of learners. As Splitter (2011, p. 497) explains:

> Participating in a CoI allows students, individually and collaboratively, to develop their own ideas and perspectives based on appropriately rigorous modes of thinking *and* against the background of a thorough understanding and appreciation of those ideas and perspectives that, having stood the test of time, may be represented as society's best view of things to date.

In this way, educators are aiming at deepening children's critical thinking skills as they facilitate a meaningful dialogue that aims at a shared understanding and also at truth. Advocates of P4C are also concerned with caring, creative and collaborative thinking skills, as students are recognised as seeking truth while being situated in a context, in a time and place. This contextual aspect to our existence does not deny the existence of shared values, and, ultimately, the CoI pursues our best understanding of things as they are currently, while remaining open to self-correction with time and as new information comes to light. The CoI follows the line of inquiry where it leads and acknowledges the pursuit of knowledge to be a process that is open, pluralistic and democratic (Winstanley, 2008).

The attitude of critical perspectivism may be educated via the CoI pedagogy and then applied to our online engagement. Our judgements and actions become ingrained the more we practise them. Factors influencing our habitual manner of responding to people and situations come from many sources, including friends, family and the social environment around us. Mass and social media and mass art are prominent sources that depict examples of behaviour that are then judged as acceptable or problematic within our society. Such depictions should, according to Nussbaum (1990; 1995) and Iris Murdoch (1970), at least in respect to narrative artworks, be truthful and fair. Yet much of our mass art promotes questionable stereotypes and dubious fear-filled stories that are purported to inform us of newsworthy facts. Ultimately, we require the skills to be able to discern fact from fiction, genuine insight from embellishment and manipulation. We similarly require these cognitive abilities and guiding moral principles to be applied when we consider with what we choose to engage, propagate and share. In the age of Web and Media 2.0, everyone is a storyteller with the ability to pitch an idea on the world stage. The CoI is designed to teach us to be critical of the ideas and beliefs we and others hold, while simultaneously being respectful towards and compassionate of the others who hold such diverse perspectives, recognising that together we form a community of people seeking the truth and a harmonious life. For those who do not seek truth or harmony, we must be able to appeal to normative values in order to judge and condemn things that may threaten our peaceful coexistence.

Once taught or modelled, and if practised, eventually a habit may form whereby people routinely engage with multiple perspectives in a critical and compassionate manner. This habit may be formed within a classroom setting or elsewhere, and one methodology by which to achieve it is the CoI. When properly facilitated, the CoI may equally be employed in a philosophy café and thus highlights the way in which public philosophy may be useful within society. Teaching people to be critically yet compassionately engaged citizens who are able to effectively negotiate multiple perspectives is a necessary skill in today's technologically connected, global world. Using philosophy as a praxis highlights the important role philosophers may take in educational as well as public spaces. Approaching philosophy as accessible, making use of ordinary language and taken to the streets, as it were, is not new or radical, yet is vital now more than ever. Furthermore, approaching philosophy in this practical and applied manner does not diminish the serious work of philosophy; nor does it undermine the academic work done in universities within philosophy departments. In fact, the philosopher as public intellectual, serving to model such critical, and, importantly, compassionate thinking skills, can complement and supplement the valuable work of philosophy done in the academy. It is my hope that such an approach would serve academic philosophy well by expanding its vocational application, along with making philosophy more inviting and inclusive, particularly for women and minorities, something the discipline sorely needs.

The stories we tell

The virtual public sphere is open in an exciting new way with ideas being discussed and debated in a transparent and engaging manner. Yet the openness of the Internet also makes it a public forum that evokes criticism and trolling. The technological tools themselves are value neutral; it is the character that employs them for constructive or destructive means which may be labelled virtuous or vicious. Social media and online sites may alter with new technological developments, yet it is the personality of individuals using such mediums that requires the focus of educators. At worst, unstructured discussion online is full of misinformation and promotes superstition and anti-scientism. It may allow for negative personal attacks or bullying. At best, it fosters genuine learning through expansive dialogue that respects those engaging in the discussion and encourages self-reflection. To foster the latter, we must train the habits of the individual, which include critical and creative thinking, the intellectual and moral virtues, discernment and compassion. Instead of dealing with concerns about social networking sites by banning their use, we ought to teach our students to engage critically with information sources so that they have the tools they'll need when out on their own in the technological world, a world that cannot be ignored or avoided without disengaging from society.

In a unique way, consumers are more connected globally and more able to make an impact on the marketplace (of ideas as well as of products and services) than ever before. The notion of consumer satisfaction has gained enormous power, with reviews and 'likes' gaining traction as such feedback has a direct impact upon industry, service providers and public intellectuals. Those using social media have direct access to famous people, experts, institutions and industries and feel empowered in that their voice is instantly heard. In the old days, a grumpy 'letter to the editor' may or may not be published. These days, if that grumpy consumer has access to the Internet, they can make their complaints known far and wide immediately. In a time when nothing is erased, this is both positive and a cause for concern.

In a truly democratic space, the positive uptake of messages such as ethical causes and charitable donations is visible as certain fads go 'viral'. Yet this is also set against the notion of 'slacktivism', which amounts to clicking 'like' on a picture of a starving child to support the cause and raise awareness for a charity, which is not the same thing as donating to assist the charity or the starving children. Raising awareness alone may not translate into ethical behaviour or actions that actually assist and impact positively on a cause. Additionally, in this populist environment, the positive aspect of the client's voice being heard is set against the negativity of the troll's voice being heard and the rise in cyber-bullying.

It appears to me that education and moderated forums can play an important role in dealing with these issues. Issues of unethical behaviour are a human problem, and what we are now seeing is the expression of such antisocial behaviour through technological mediums. An important issue that must be considered by those engaging in a critically perspectival manner (online or elsewhere) is whether or not all opinions are entitled to be heard within a liberal democracy. In chapter six, I consider whether philosophers may encourage critical thinking and compassionate responses beyond the classroom environment, and to that end I examine the role of the philosopher as a public intellectual. It is worth exploring whether philosophical thinking skills can assist to set public debates on the right path via the use of good argumentation and the application of critical thinking skills such as avoiding fallacies and addressing the topic, not the person. In modelling such respectful and yet critical engagement with ideas within a public forum, philosophers may play an important role in clarifying arguments under debate within society, while also elevating (ideally morally as well as intellectually) the level of public discourse. Obviously, such a role may be played by people other than philosophers, yet I believe there is certainly space for more public intellectuals, including philosophers to speak up within online and other public forums.

One central concern is the idea that, when communication is mediated and online, people sometimes forget that they are interacting with whole, embodied, real others. This is where the idea of compassion becomes of paramount importance. It is not simply critical, analytical and rational thinking skills that good citizens need to possess, it is also rational emotions such as compassion and the ability to work and play in a collaborative setting alongside others. Therefore, while there is certainly the need for critical discernment when sorting through the information and misinformation abundant online, there is the need to respect others as thinking and feeling human beings. It is particularly obvious online in a global, decontextualised space that we need to accommodate pluralism in the sense that we will discover multiple perspectives and conflicting attitudes amongst people. However, we must also recognise the normative aspect of shared human values and virtues that are common to all. We ought to resist the collapse into relativism, even as we aim at tolerance, inclusion and diversity (Bleazby, 2011; Golding, 2011; MacIntyre, 2007).

In our contemporary, technological society with multiple perspectives coming 'at' us constantly, the attitude of critical perspectivism allows moral agents to critically evaluate information and figure out the appropriately rational and compassionate response. Storytelling is a powerful medium by which one may communicate ideas, express morality and influence others. Value judgements are embedded in our language, and the words we use often imply or presume certain ethical evaluations. It is storytelling accompanied by images that explains the power of mass art and social media to convey information quickly, to large audiences, using few words. While I cannot quantify the impact or effect such media has in society, I argue that we need to be educating people to engage constructively with such media wherever possible. Lost in a sea of information and misinformation, we need to critically discern between multiple sources of information with diverse aims, intentions and messages. If such education can commence at a young age with school-aged children, then these digital natives will grow up with the necessary skills that will assist them to negotiate the online world and prepare them for dealing with future technological developments.

Conclusion

Whether for good or bad, mass art and media undeniably have an immense presence and impact upon society, in part simply due to the fact that mass artworks and media frequently command mass audiences. As such, examining the role that such media plays in society from an ethical perspective is a worthwhile enterprise. The power and potential of mass art and media cannot be denied; whether particular instances and examples are evaluated as negative or positive, it is agreed that they have the potential to have a strong impact. In this book, my concern is on how moral agents should engage critically and compassionately with information received, online or otherwise. I suggest that such agents will treat others well, according to shared moral values and norms, while seeking truth and sound evidence for their beliefs. To this end, teaching people critical thinking skills and offering opportunities for them to practise compassionate habits is vital, and this may occur within CoIs that prompt intelligent discernment, an open-minded analytical approach while fostering creativity, caring and tolerance. Such virtues are necessary to inform one's moral character and are applicable to the art of living, particularly in a modern technological society in which it is all but impossible to escape passive or active engagement with multiple sources of information that are mass-produced, distributed and consumed. As this is the case, critical perspectivism is useful in order to critically digest ideas and messages that are omnipresent in society.

In highlighting the importance of critical perspectivism in today's society, I also illuminate a possible role for the philosopher as public intellectual. Without detracting from the important work done by philosophers within the academy, teaching and researching within universities and similar institutions, philosophers, given their relevant thinking skills, also have a role to play in public spaces, moderated online forums and within schools. Including philosophers in public debates and discussions, as well as facilitating CoIs both within and outside of school classroom settings, would benefit society. In this way, philosophers can serve as role models for good thinking skills and for teacher-training, among other forms of professional development, as well as generally add a critical and yet compassionate voice (ideally) to issues of importance under public scrutiny and debate.

Philosophical thinking skills will support the attitude of critical perspectivism, and it is the habituation of this attitude that will result in ethically motivated, democratic citizens. Critically and compassionately engaged members of society will necessarily be engaged socially, politically, economically and morally because we are social creatures who live and work in communities. Critical perspectivism is set against the backdrop of the moral agent as a global citizen. Technology allows us to be more connected than ever previously, and thus we have a responsibility to consider the plight of others and to recognise ourselves as shared inhabitants of planet earth. The global citizen is compassionate as well as critical, rational but practical and open to new information and ideas. This citizen will be an ethical consumer and promote and support sustainability. We cannot keep using the earth's resources in a utilitarian manner without consideration of the global consequences. One who engages critical perspectivism will surely recognise that each of us has a responsibility to live ethically, as do governments and policy makers. Thus, it is worth considering what we are advocating for through our choices of consumption, which include the portrayal of values through images, narratives, comments and, yes, even advertising. The global citizen needs to ask questions such as, 'whose voices are we championing when we engage with certain media, art and news?' 'Which images of men, women, children, minorities, cultures, stereotypes etc. do we use and re-use and what kinds of discrimination does this perpetuate?' In this book, I claim that we should adopt and teach an attitude that I name critical perspectivism in the hope that it will have a positive moral effect upon both the individual as well as our global society. Such claims ultimately culminate in support of the notion of the global citizen as defined and defended by Peter Singer (2002), Naomi Klein (2014) and Martha Nussbaum (2012).

While it can be argued that not all mass art or media texts encourage audiences or users to think for themselves, if the form of mass art or media allows for artworks and texts that inspire thought and perhaps even ethical action, society could benefit from such mass-produced and widely distributed stories, images and messages. I am interested in the link of mass art and media to education in order to encourage critical thinking, creative reflection, tolerance and understanding when it comes to notions of difference. Critical perspectivism offers individuals a way to effectively interpret and judge information that comes from the many sources of information that surround us, particularly the mass art and media realms. The influence of such multimedia is unavoidable in our society and to make positive use of it we must engage critically with such media as well as the moral messages contained therein. Critical perspectivism can thus be linked to moral education and the study of philosophy whereby adults and children may practise adopting an active, critical and compassionate attitude towards others with whom they engage, bearing in mind that the diversity of ideas does not disprove the existence of shared human values. In seeking truth, philosophers may facilitate communities of inquiry using Socratic dialogue techniques to encourage people to think rationally as well as ethically. Critical perspectivism is an attitude that may be taught and practised within educational spaces, such as within a community of inquiry, and then adopted and employed online or face-to-face.

References

Adorno, T. W., & Horkheimer, M. (1997). *Dialectic of Enlightenment*. London: Verso.

Albers, P., & Harste, J. C. (2007). The arts, new literacies, and multimodality. *English Education*, *40*(1), 6–20.

Benjamin, W. (1969). The work of art in the age of mechanical reproduction (H. Zorn, trans.). In H. Arendt (Ed.), *Illuminations* (pp. 217–252). New York: Schocken Books.

Bleazby, J. (2011). Overcoming relativism and absolutism: Dewey's ideals of truth and meaning in philosophy for children. *Educational Philosophy and Theory*, *43*(5), 453–466.

Boyd, D., & Ellison, N. (2008). Social network sites: Definition, history, and scholarship. *Journal of Computer-Mediated Communication*, *13*(1), 210–230.

Burgh, G., Field, T., & Freakley, M. (2006). *Ethics and the community of inquiry: Education for deliberative democracy*. South Melbourne: Thomson.

Cam, P. (Ed.). (1993/1997). *Thinking stories*. Alexandria, NSW, Australia: Hale & Iremonger.

Cam, P. (2006). *Twenty thinking tools.* Camberwell, Victoria, Australia: ACER.

Collingwood, R. G. (1938). *The principles of art.* Oxford: Clarendon Press.

Cook, J., & Lewandowsky, S. (2011). *The debunking handbook.* St. Lucia, Australia: The University of Queensland. November 5. ISBN 978-0-646-56812-6. Retrieved from http://sks.to/debunk

Cope, B., & Kalantzis, M. (Eds.). (2000). *Multiliteracies: Literacy learning and the design of social futures.* London: Routledge.

Deleuze, G. (1986). *Cinema I: The movement-image* (H. Tomlinson & B. Habberjam, trans.). Minneapolis: University of Minnesota Press.

Deleuze, G. (1989). *Cinema II: The time-image.* Minneapolis: University of Minnesota Press.

Dewey, J. (1997). *How we think.* Mineola, NY: Dover Publications.

Dewey, J. (2008). Democracy and education, 1916. *Studies in Education, 5*(1/2), 87–95.

D'Olimpio, L. (2014). Thoughts on film: Critically engaging with both Adorno and Benjamin. *Educational Philosophy and Theory, 47*(6), 622–637.

Frampton, D. (2006). *Filmosophy.* London: Wallflower Press.

Golding, C. (2011). The many faces of constructivist discussion. *Educational Philosophy and Theory, 43*(5), 467–483.

Golding, C., Gurr, D., & Hinton, L. (2012). Leadership for creating a thinking school at Buranda State School. *Leading & Managing, 18*(1), 91–106.

Greenberg, C. (1971). *Art and culture: critical essays.* Boston: Beacon Press.

Kalantzis, M., & Cope, B. (2012). *New learning: Elements of a science education* (2nd ed.). Cambridge: Cambridge University Press. Supplemented by *New Learning: Transformational Designs for Pedagogy and Assessment* website. Retrieved from newlearningonline.com

Kennedy, K. (2015). Practicing philosophy of childhood: Teaching in the (r)evolutionary mode. *Journal of Philosophy in Schools, 2*(1), 4–17. Retrieved from www.ojs.unisa.edu.au/index.php/jps/article/view/1099

Klein, N. (2014). *This changes everything: Capitalism vs. the climate.* New York: Simon & Schuster.

Lenhart, A. (2015). *Teens, social media, & technology overview 2015.* Washington: Pew Research Centre. Retrieved August 11, 2016, from www.pewInternet.org/2015/04/09/teens-social-media-technology-2015/

Lipman, M. (2003). *Thinking in education* (2nd ed.). Cambridge: Cambridge University Press.

MacDonald, D. (1963). *Against the American grain.* London: Victor Gollanz.

MacIntyre, A. (2007). *After virtue: A study in moral theory.* Notre Dame, IN: University of Notre Dame Press.

√ Marwick, A. E. (2013). *Status update: Celebrity, publicity, and branding in the social media age.* New Haven: Yale University Press.

Millett, S., & Tapper, A. (2012). Benefits of collaborative philosophical inquiry in schools. *Educational Philosophy and Theory, 44*(5), 546–567.

Mulhall, S. (2002). *On film.* London: Routledge.

Murdoch, I. (1970). *The sovereignty of good.* London: Routledge.

Nussbaum, M. C. (1987). Finely aware and richly responsible: Literature and the moral imagination. In A. J. Cascardi (Ed.), *Literature and the questions of philosophy* (pp. 169–191). Baltimore: The John Hopkins University Press.

Nussbaum, M. C. (1990). *Love's knowledge.* Oxford: Oxford University Press.

Nussbaum, M. C. (1995). *Poetic justice: The literary imagination and public life*. Boston: Beacon Press.

Nussbaum, M. C. (2012). *The new religious intolerance: Overcoming the politics of fear in an anxious age*. Cambridge: The Belknap Press of Harvard University Press.

Sensis Pty Ltd. (2015). *Sensis social media report May 2015: How Australian people and businesses are using social media*. Melbourne. Retrieved August 11, 2016, from www.sensis.com.au/assets/PDFdirectory/Sensis_Social_Media_Report_2015.pdf

Singer, P. (2002). *One World: The Ethics of Globalisation*. Melbourne: Text Publishing Company.

Splitter, L. (2011). Identity, citizenship and moral education. *Educational Philosophy and Theory, 43*(5), 484–505.

Splitter, L., & Sharp, A. M. (1995). *Teaching for better thinking: The classroom community of inquiry*. Melbourne: ACER.

Vansieleghem, N., & Kennedy, D. (Eds.). (2012). *Philosophy for children in transition: Problems and prospects*. The Journal of Philosophy of Education Book Series. West Sussex: Wiley-Blackwell.

Wartenberg, T. E. (2007). *Thinking on screen: Film as philosophy*. London: Routledge.

Winstanley, C. (2008). Philosophy and the development of critical thinking. In M. Hand & C. Winstanley (Eds.), *Philosophy in schools* (pp. 85–95). London: Continuum.

1 Critical perspectivism

Critical perspectivism is an ethical attitude that may be applied to processing and understanding information received from multiple sources, including multimedia. It is an attitude that requires a moral agent to be critical and compassionate. To be critically perspectival means to approach information in a critically engaged way, seeking the truth by checking claims for evidence and resting belief upon sound arguments that are reflected upon logically. Yet it is more than this, as it also includes the understanding that others with opinions, beliefs and agendas different from our own are fully fleshed out human beings much like us. This understanding that others are *like us* in important respects, aiming at living a good life with a sense of meaning or purpose, means that even when they present claims that are biased or incorrect, we ought to approach them with compassion, even when we must, at times and only when appropriate, also be sceptical of the stories they tell us and, perhaps, even condemn them for the things they say and do. While compassionate and allowing for multiple perspectives, critical perspectivism also allows for moral judgment and seeks the best possible answer for how we should live our lives and treat others. This seeming tension between being caring and critical is accommodated when we acknowledge the pluralism of perspectives in the world and affirm the existence of shared values and objective truth even while noting the contextual and individual differences that exist amongst persons and their experiences.

Critical perspectivism is particularly applied to multimedia in this book given that contemporary technology allows us almost infinite and instantaneous access to various news stories, images, messages and voices available to us online. Of course we also receive multiple perspectives and arguments, opinions and images face-to-face as we traverse the streets and encounter others in our everyday lives, or similarly as we engage with narrative artworks and learn about fictional characters, their thoughts, feelings and behaviour. Critical perspectivism is applicable to these instances as well. In this chapter, critical perspectivism will be detailed as an attitude one may employ that is relevant to various scenarios.

A primary focus of this book is how critical perspectivism may be particularly useful when applied to various things online. This does not exclude using it elsewhere, and I will consider it in relation to mass art, narrative artworks, mass media and broadcast news, social media as well as with respect to face-to-face interaction.

Critical perspectivism, on this account, is also relevant to interpersonal exchanges such as those that occur within an educative setting like a philosophy for children classroom that is running a community of inquiry dialogue. Yet it is a feature of contemporary society that much of our knowledge is sourced online, many times in an interactive manner as we access wikis, social networking sites, blogs and opinion pages alongside more traditional online versions of dictionaries, encyclopedias, broadcast news reported by journalists and research papers written by academics. The online media will tailor, limit and disseminate such information and images in particular ways suited to ease of access and widespread dissemination of information by multiple, global users. Much of this information will further be shaped and structured, and often distorted, by inbuilt restrictions of the site such as Twitter's 140 characters (plus a link!) per Tweet or the algorithm that determines which Facebook stories will appear at the top of your newsfeed. Most online sites will also have an interest in attracting an increasing number of users and repeat visitors, aiming at lengthening the amount of time users spend on their sites as well as how widely they perpetuate information they have discovered via that site. Such engagement and interest will be measured by likes, shares and comments; all capable of measurement and review by the relevant stakeholders who then determine what changes will be made to these sites, which, in turn, affects how people receive and transmit information. It is precisely because the information (including images) we encounter contains implicit or explicit social, political and moral messages that it needs to be approached actively and critically with a caring response to real-life others. This critically reflective attitude (critical perspectivism) also needs to be focussed on the media platforms and sites with which we are engaging, to consider the contextual features of the structures that provide and prohibit knowledge.

I argue that critical perspectivism, the attitude of being critical and compassionately engaged with multiple perspectives, will assist anyone using the technological tools that are ubiquitous in everyday life. Building upon my analysis of Nussbaum's 'loving attitude', which will be articulated further in chapter two, critical perspectivism helps viewers and users of social media, art and mass art, media and various news and information outlets to be critically and ethically discerning of the information and narratives they are being told, while also compassionately aware of the fact that the others with whom one engages are much like oneself. This attitude accepts that there will be various perspectives presented on any given subject, yet this pluralism does not result in a denial of shared values because, despite personal, cultural and social variance, there is still a shared common humanity and corresponding virtues.

In this way, critical perspectivism is different from Nietzsche's concept of 'perspectivism', which arguably collapses into relativism. At the end of *On The Genealogy of Morality* (1994/1887), Nietzsche writes, "There is only a seeing from a perspective, only a "knowing" from a perspective, and the more emotions we express over a thing, the more eyes, different eyes, we train on the same thing, the more complete will be our "idea" of that thing, our "objectivity"." While this is taken to dismiss objective truth, this quote is within the section entitled 'What is the Meaning of Ascetic Ideals?' and makes reference to life affirming rather than life denying values. Such values are arguably artistic and affective (Dionysian) as well as cognitive and rational (Apollonian). It is possible to apply a virtue ethics lens to Nietzsche's account of morality, and this may result in a pluralistic account of morality rather than a radical subjectivism. Although the purpose of this chapter is not to delve deeply into the philosophy of Nietzsche, it is worth reflecting on the use of the term 'perspectivism' as it is associated with Nietzsche, despite my different application of the term.

Specifically, I employ a virtue ethics framework. In light of this, it is worth noting that Christine Swanton (2015) has read Nietzsche as a virtue ethicist, excavating his virtuous egoism and further arguing that the virtues are, and should be understood as, pluralistic and contextual or, as she terms it, "response dependent", in such a way that "acknowledges the complexity of *human* responsiveness to the world" (Swanton, 2003, p. 23). Understood in this way, the notion of trying to adopt multiple perspectives, including perspectives other than one's own, is not too far removed from the advantages Nussbaum sees literary artworks afford their attentive readers. Indeed, Nietzsche's early writing, The *Birth of Tragedy* (1872), defends the role of the arts *as a necessary supplement to logic and science; the aesthetic is another realm of knowing* (p. 51). Referring to Nietzsche's *Birth of Tragedy*, Nussbaum (1998) notes "[t]he arts show us that we can have order and discipline and meaning and logic from within ourselves: we do not have to choose between belief in god and empty chaos" (p. 59). Imaginatively engaging with various perspectives in a sympathetic manner, therefore, can lead to a more holistic understanding of a concept or situation.

Yet, even taking into consideration Nussbaum and Swanton's charitable readings of Nietzsche, there remains, as with other works often classified as existentialist, the tendency towards relativism and subjectivism that allows for Nietzsche's 'will to power' to manifest in ways that may override any shared social conventions and mores. Nietzsche depicts humans as creators or artists who are encouraged to affirm life as they shape their own lives to form a masterpiece. While this is a positive and constructive idea, there is no obvious limitation within Nietzsche's writings as to the shaping of one's weaknesses whereby the artist reworks weaknesses into strengths or qualities that are aesthetically pleasing to oneself. Indeed, the artist may simply adopt a different perspective or point of view in seeking to 'delight' their own eye – and they need not adopt the moral point of view reflected within society. This imagery of the artist is present not only in *Birth of Tragedy*, it recurs later in Nietzsche's aphorism §290 'One thing is needful' in *The Gay Science* (1974/1882):

> *One thing is needful.* – To "give style" to one's character – a great and rare art! It is practiced by those who survey all the strengths and weaknesses of their nature and then fit them into an artistic plan until every one of them appears as art and reason and even weaknesses delight the eye.

In this way, the major criticism of the approach to 'living one's life as an artist' is that the authentic life is extremely subjective. If I am the artist creating my life to be a masterpiece that suits my taste, there does not seem to be anything stopping me from being selfish, which erodes any sense of morality. While I have elsewhere argued that this subjectivism may be overcome by augmenting Nietzsche's aestheticism with an Aristotelian framework (see D'Olimpio & Teschers, 2017), for the purposes of critical perspectivism, Nietzsche's perspectivism alone is insufficient. Firstly, Nietzsche's perspectivism is not compassionate enough, particularly given that Nietzsche views sympathy as a sign of weakness. This is evident in much of his writings, but see, for instance, *The Gay Science* aphorism §338 'The Will to Suffering and the Compassionate' in which pity is said to be a source of danger, compassion is said to be a sign of weakness and suffering is said to be personal and incomprehensible to others. In contrast to this, compassion (directed towards others as well as oneself) is vital to my account of critical perspectivism. Secondly, Nietzsche's perspectivism is not critical enough, as the only critic that ultimately matters, on his account, is that of the individual Subject him (or her) self. Critical perspectivism must take into account the perspectives of others and use these to critique and interrogate assumptions, claims and beliefs.

I assume as an epistemological starting point that objective truths and facts about the world exist, even if these facts must be understood by individuals from an embodied perspective. I also allow that sometimes, in practise, the best 'answer' humans can hope for may be a tentatively settled pragmatic answer, particularly in real-world contexts. This does not deny shared human values or truth or wisdom (*phronesis*), rather it affirms it. Therefore, while my attitude of critical perspectivism is different to Nietzsche's 'perspectivism', the use of the word (perspectivism) acknowledges the embodied point of view humans must adopt, and thus also nods to the inclusion of affect alongside rationality. In this way, critical perspectivism may find a brief moment of sympathy with an aspect of Nietzsche's ascetic approach in that both offer a critique of the pure propositional search for a transcendental, objectively rational epistemology that is removed from an empirical grounding or contextual application in the real world. Nietzsche's approach allows for philosophical and moral truths to be explored, represented and critiqued through narrative artworks and not solely through philosophical papers that express their arguments in standard form. This is best exemplified in Nietzsche's own literary style, such as his use of aphorisms and what may be read as dramatic soliloquies. While such artistic flourishes seem unusual when considered alongside the works of twentieth- and twenty-first–century philosophers employed by the academy, we only have to remember Plato's dialogues and use of imagery and symbolism in thought experiments such as the cave analogy to see that such devices have historically appeared in philosophical texts. These themes will be further explored in chapters two and three, where the links between philosophy and literature, mass art and film are investigated.

Critical perspectivism highlights the importance of taking on the perspective of others, and seeking to understand them and their experiences in the world while also acknowledging shared human values and experiences. It does not suggest radical postmodernism or subjectivism, whereby we are somehow trapped in our own view of the world and unable to take on other points of view or learn from the experiences of others. On the contrary, critical perspectivism acknowledges shared values and virtues, a shared world and shared meaning that does allow for objective truth and facts about the world, a world in which human beings strive to flourish. The attitude of critical perspectivism requires compassionate and imaginative engagement with specific scenarios and others, but also critical distance, while aiming to see the objective whole.

A supplementary moral attitude

Critical perspectivism may be considered as a supplementary moral attitude, much like Martha Nussbaum's well-known version of ethical attention, her 'loving' attitude (Nussbaum, 1990). I consider Nussbaum's 'loving attitude' as a cousin of critical perspectivism. Both are based upon a virtue ethics framework, as they defend a particular character disposition a moral agent may adopt that allows for a contextual ethical response to information received and others encountered which also has room for rational emotions such as compassion. In this way, both critical perspectivism and Nussbaum's 'loving attitude' offer a useful supplementary moral attitude that fills in the 'gaps' left by other rule-based moral theories such as deontology and utilitarianism. This is not to discard the place for universal rules that may be enshrined in law (i.e. human rights, for instance). As a supplementary theory, critical perspectivism may be seen as an attitude an individual moral agent adopts when faced with multiple stories and sources of information which need to be processed and responded to or acted upon. The critically perspectival attitude may take into account the feelings of others, their context, as well as the ethically relevant features of the situation or information such as those highlighted by other rule-based moral theories. As such, the ethical judgements supported by normative moral theories such as deontology or utilitarianism will be considered as only one option amongst many that the moral agent can take into consideration. The ethical agent will consider duty, intention, the act itself, the consequences of the act and the relationships amongst those who are affected by the moral decision (i.e. the stakeholders). But, ultimately, the attitude of critical perspectivism sees the one adopting the attitude take an all-things-considered approach to figuring out what to do and what to believe. In this way, any deontological or consequentialist considerations therefore offer one among multiple perspectives which should be taken into critical and compassionate consideration.

At a normative or even metaethical level, the main moral theories all have different starting points or supreme normative principals from which a moral decision is made. Utilitarianism is based on outcome, while deontology is based on intention or duty; virtue ethics is based on character and rational emotions such as compassion, whilst relativism uses personal opinion or, in the case of cultural relativism, subjective cultural norms. Thus, when applying one of these theories to an argument, the premises and conclusion will be informed by the particular theory employed. Even when such arguments are logically sound and valid because their premises lead to a rational conclusion, the arguments will differ to the extent which different theories are used in their defence. To illustrate, in order to assess morality, utilitarian arguments will consider outcomes, deontological arguments will consider the universalisation of an act or inviolable principles, virtue ethics arguments will consider whether the person of moral character would act in this way, and cultural relativism will consider what is culturally acceptable for their community. However, as these theories base their premises on different normative or evaluative concepts, they conflict. As such, the theories are conceptually incommensurable (MacIntyre, 2008). It is the case that most people, when making moral decisions, consider factors that pertain to each of these theories. Thus, if proponents of utilitarianism, for instance, believe that moral agents should be perfectly consistent and only ever consider the consequences of actions, they necessarily omit considering actions in themselves and the intentions of a moral agent, factors that moral agents will take into account *alongside* potential outcomes of their decisions.

When people make moral decisions, they, knowingly or unknowingly, often use a mixture of utilitarian and deontological reasoning along with virtue ethics (including ethics of care), as well as considering some subjective or culturally relevant factors. This claim is supported by the research conducted by Ciprian (2015), who investigated how members of Australian Animal Ethics Committees (AECs) make decisions with respect to various scenarios regarding the use of animals for the purposes of scientific experimentation. Ciprian employed three different approaches to support the hypothesis that members of AECs use a mixture of different ethical theories when making and justifying their decisions as to whether it is morally correct to approve or deny an application for animal experimentation. The experimental approaches analysed included discourse analysis of written texts and the discussion within mock AECs as well as a multidimensional ethics scale that was issued as a survey to test which ethical theories are used by veterinarians, scientists, animal welfare representatives and lay people to assess animal experimentation as ethical. Ciprian concluded that AEC members (represented by the four stakeholder groups above) predominantly used utilitarian reasoning; however, there were also instances of deontological reasoning, appeals to virtues and rational emotions such as care alongside relativistic claims and justifications such as appeals to personal experiences and likes or dislikes, as well as cultural preferences such as those pertaining to animals seen as 'pets'. Such seeming inconsistency may worry those wishing to defend morality, yet I am reassured that we need not lose hope for the role of moral judgement and the existence of shared normative values. In fact, the strength of critical and caring decision making applied contextually is that such ethical decisions respond to real situations which are rich and complex, varying in moral intensity and impact. Furthermore, critical perspectivism can assist us to take account of the point of view from which others are viewing the issue under discussion.

In light of the inconsistency of moral agents' decision making, enshrining moral laws into legal rules or human rights may be considered a good idea. Yet there is still the variance in considering how to apply and punish such laws which change over time and from place to place. For instance, attitudes towards, and associated laws pertaining to, free speech or self defence (including the carrying of weapons) differ from Australia to the USA. However, the morality or legality or political nature of laws is beyond the scope of this book. What is of central concern to critical perspectivism is how individuals respond, morally, to what they see, read and hear. With the advancements in our technology, we are seeing, reading and hearing more than ever previously. Any rights we may have or wish to defend will also apply online, yet these will be more difficult to negotiate as we enter a global space that is not bound in the usual ways by national legislation or even shared cultural understanding (consider the limitations in certain countries surrounding what citizens are allowed to access online for instance). Yes, laws and rules governing, for instance, free speech also apply in the online domain, yet, as we enter a global space, these also become much more difficult to enforce if we are worried about preventing harm. I will not delve into the limitations of free speech here or how such rights should be enforced. At this point, I simply wish to acknowledge the on-going debate surrounding such issues, which also apply to online forums. The main focus of the supplementary moral attitude I defend takes seriously the fact that we are operating within a global world with access to multiple, variant points of view. The moral agent who adopts a critically perspectival attitude will recognise that, for instance, when discussing freedom of speech with their (virtual or otherwise) friend in America, their friend may well hold different assumptions and experiences than if they had been raised in Australia. Recognising such differences is not inconsistent with a push for moral rules, laws, or the seeking of universal rights that pertain to everyone, even where they are interpreted differently in different places at different times. Similarly, critical perspectivism as a supplementary moral attitude is not antagonistic to other normative moral theories such as utilitarianism or deontology.

The work done by a critically perspectival attitude is that of the individual, the moral agent who is taking in information and needs to decide what to do or how to react or respond in an ethical manner. This attitude may be trained and cultivated, learnt and then habituated, until it is a reflexive response to others both face-to-face as well as online. The ways in which critical perspectivism may be educated will be the focus of chapter five. It is important to note that, even if moral agents are rational, they will disagree as to whether or not euthanasia is moral, whether sharks should be culled, or whether abortion is permissible. Such moral disagreement is reasonable (see Hand, 2014), and some controversial moral issues may be unsolvable in the sense that reasonable people will disagree as to what is the right thing to do in these applied ethics scenarios, and even where they agree they may disagree as to why they believe that to be the right thing. It is for these reasons that critical perspectivism is necessary as an attitude the moral agent can employ in recognition of such diversity and variance, even while holding that some moral rules are universal albeit not uncontroversial.

Caring

I shall initially briefly consider the loving attitude of ethical attention before analysing how critical perspectivism is a more useful attitude to adopt, particularly with respect to multimedia sources of information. Influenced by the ethics of care theorists Simone Weil (1978) and Nel Noddings (1984), as well as by Iris Murdoch (1970), Martha Nussbaum defends an attitude of ethical attention that is a compassionate and loving attention directed towards the particulars of a situation whereby the morally relevant factors are first discerned and then attended to. Nussbaum expresses the notion of ethical attention in a theoretically rigorous and plausible manner by arguing that we need to take into consideration the embodied humanness of our nature, which includes the intellect, appropriate emotions and our imagination. Thus the loving attitude to which Nussbaum refers is a moral attitude aided by appropriate emotions which have a cognitive element (Nussbaum, 2001), and the imagination that enables us to empathise with others. We can learn by seeing things from alternative perspectives by imaginatively placing ourselves in that situation, even if we have not had the experience ourselves. What may be underemphasised on this account is the notion of a 'critical eye'. If we fall into the perspective of another too deeply, without retaining enough critical detachment, we may feel their situation too strongly, such that it adversely affects our own well-being. For instance, if we worry about them, the situation or the cause *too much*, we may be overwhelmed by our care-based feelings and we may also be less objective when deciding how best to respond to the facts of the case.

Of course Nussbaum may respond to this challenge by saying that a case of 'too much' sympathetic attention may be described as 'excessive' and moral agents should be aiming for the golden mean (mid-point between that which is excessive and that which is deficient). Yet this account of a loving attitude will also have to acknowledge individual character: some people will be more sympathetic than others. As such, the golden mean is not entirely useful in that it does not explicitly illuminate what the moral agent ought to do. The vagueness or flexibility of the golden mean is an asset as well as a hindrance, precisely because, for example, the loving attitude is a guiding principle that may be applied to a context or situation, but then leaves it up to the individual moral agent to work out how they must appropriately respond in a loving way. Critical perspectivism faces some similar challenges to the loving attitude outlined by Nussbaum, in that individuals may be more or less critical and/or compassionate. However, critical perspectivism solves the problem of excessive sentiment and balances it with a critical eye that ensures that such an attitude is more appropriate and useful, particularly when dealing with information, images and others online. Multiple perspectives have to be considered in order to gain the best view of the whole situation. In order to make accurate moral judgements, discernment is crucial. Such moral discernment includes emotional as well as cognitive perspicuity. As will become apparent, while both Nussbaum's loving attitude and critical perspectivism include cognitive discernment employed alongside rational emotions such as compassion, critical perspectivism is not quite as vague or subjective as Nussbaum's loving attitude.

Nussbaum is a neo-Aristotelian virtue ethicist who supplements a virtue framework with a particular (loving) attitude and mode of caring. This loving attitude that takes into account situational factors enhances moral decision making partly by helping one to discern which virtues are applicable and how to apply them. In this way, a moral response is a prudent response, and it must be trained and practised until it becomes a habitual response. This loving attitude invites us, as moral agents, to empathise with one another and learn by seeing things from alternative perspectives by imaginatively placing ourselves in that situation. The benefit of a theory such as Nussbaum's is that it counters the problematic of a deontic approach which makes use of a rational, unemotional motivating factor of 'duty' to judge the morally correct course of action or that of the utilitarian who seeks to maximise utility by weighing up consequences whereby each human being counts as a 'unit' of measurement with the aim or end being the 'greater good' or some satisfaction of the majority of individual preferences. A utilitarian modus operandi or Kantian moral framework will sometimes result in a counter-intuitive, cold-hearted morality that is detached and abstractly perfect. Such moral theories are perfect only in theory, as a potential for which flawed individuals may strive in practice. In contrast, Nussbaum posits a far more realistic vision of embodied, passionate human beings who are also, at the same time, moral (Richardson, 1998, p. 257). This is important as, Nussbaum claims, "an ethics of impartial respect for human dignity will fail to engage real human beings unless they are capable of entering imaginatively into the lives of distant others and to have emotions related to that participation" (Nussbaum, 1995, p. xvi – preface). In other words, Kant's notion of duty by itself is not enough to motivate moral action, even if we are able to rationally discern the morally relevant features of a situation. And before duty can be done, one must know what it is that one should do; knowing that one should be kind does not immediately inform us as to *how* to be kind or practise kindness. However, according to Kant, one must know one's duty and emotion may interfere with either knowing (seeing clearly) or acting upon one's duty. In contrast, a virtue framework includes the emotions as a part of our moral decision-making capacity as human beings, allowing the *right kinds* of emotions to appropriately motivate us to perform the moral act. The virtue ethicist highlights the importance of prudence and practical wisdom (*phronesis*) in leading a flourishing life (*Eudaimonia*).

However, Nussbaum's loving ethical attention alone also seems limited if we are simply empathising with another in order to understand the situation in which they are in and how they feel about it, while not being appropriately critical or sceptical. It must be noted that Nussbaum is not referring to blind love; the loving attitude is also reasonable. She refers to the respect and love that operates between human beings, allowing for both rational and affective responses. There is a slight tension here, a tension that is also reflected in critical perspectivism, namely, that love draws us together in order to help each other, and respect encourages us to keep a certain distance (Kant, 1983, p. 453). For Nussbaum, it is situational discernment that is required to ascertain, case by case, what is the moral thing to do. Such a rule of action cannot be generalised, as our moral discernment and perception must be applied in each slightly different case. Notably, this differs from Kant's sense of respectful, universalised duty. Henry Richardson acknowledges the worry that Nussbaum's 'moral point of view' is a far riskier version than Kant's moral theory due to the required improvisation whereby 'improvisation' here refers to the role the imagination plays in moral decision making. Richardson also examines the concern that Nussbaum's increasingly universal concerns (for instance, for the rights of women, particularly in developing countries – see Nussbaum, 2000) may change the nature of her loving attitude whereby, upon her theory, love and respect work harmoniously together, yet when directed at universals more than particulars, this attitude may not be 'love' anymore (Richardson, 1998, p. 259). Yet Richardson replies to both of these criticisms, arguing that the accounts of love and respect in Nussbaum's writings are reconcilable as compassionate moral attitudes, namely, love that is attached to particulars and the more detached and benevolent respect that may be applied to universals or philanthropy.

Nussbaum's conception of love is morally and humanly beneficial insofar as it does the binding between particular and generalised (moral) scenarios, as opposed to Kant's sense of duty. "On her account, love underwrites a discernment of particulars that amounts to an intimate form of respect. Respect, by contrast, demands of us a response to distant people that is less tepid than a general and distance-diluted philanthropy" (Richardson, 1998, p. 259). Thus, Nussbaum's compassionate attitude enables us to care for people across the world, as well as those nearby with whom we have specific attachments. Certainly, Nussbaum realises the importance of an objective standard by which situational difference can be evaluated and she explicitly refutes relativism as a desirable moral theory (Nussbaum, 2000, pp. 41–51). This is important, as she wishes to promote civil liberties and act on moral norms, norms that moral relativism denies (Nussbaum, 2000, p. 55).

Thus, Nussbaum's supplementary moral theory promotes a compassionate attitude to cultural minorities in particular, encouraging social institutions to work ethically and humanely. Yet the *critical* element is also required, as acknowledged by Richardson and inadequately accounted for by Nussbaum's mode of ethical attention. Her objective list of universals provides standing principles, or moral guidelines by which we can judge the individual contexts, yet each context involves the appropriate use of compassion and discernment in order to accurately ascertain what needs to be done. Such discerning what is the best thing to do involves understanding the facts of the situation while also imaginatively engaging with the perspective of another or others. This skill set of intellectual and moral discernment, care and imaginative positioning is also required when access to the perspective of others is mediated through technology and received online. Yet, in such cases, it becomes increasingly obvious that the critical eye must also be activated, and critical perspectivism is the attitude we need in order to ascertain what the right thing to do is and then to apply this appropriate judgement.

Critical perspectivism

Critical perspectivism is an attitude that explores multiple perspectives, instead of simply emotionally engaging with another's viewpoint or uncritically adopting an alternative perspective. As an attitude we can practice and ultimately employ, critical perspectivism encourages us to challenge what we see, the information we receive, to judge its truth value and moral import, and consider how it applies to our lives. When we are being critically perspectival, we are analysing the information and images we receive in everyday life, particularly stories and bite-sized pieces of information that bombard us as soon as we log online or use social media or switch on a news programme. By evaluating different perspectives that constantly surround us with the aim of getting closer to the truth and the facts of a situation, we are actively engaged in the process of deciding what to believe and what to value. Such judgements inform and influence behaviour, including how we treat or respond to others. The intention of the moral agent is to get as close as possible to an objective whole or a more realistic picture of the way things are. It may be that some situations appear to be, or, in some instances, actually 'are' different to each person (given that ideology can shape one's interpretation of the world) and thus a sense of 'how things are' includes understanding the pluralism and multiple perspectives that may be available in any given scenario. Being able to make a wise, informed decision requires being able to mediate and understand as well as evaluate, and not just tolerate, diversity (as argued for by Herbert Marcuse, 1965/1969). If we fail to understand, other virtues such as tolerance become particularly pertinent to a flourishing society. Nussbaum and Murdoch are correct in that the imagination is a necessary tool for us to use to engage with others and adopt different perspectives. I add that we must also be critical, yet not cold-heartedly so, of these different perspectives.

By supplementing Nussbaum's loving attitude with a more pronounced critical eye, the moral agent seeks to be critical as well as compassionate. The caring response is directed towards real-life others, even when these others are met or conversed with only online. The critical eye is aimed at the information being received, particularly when it is technologically mediated or presented as unbiased fact. The critical eye is likely to be even more prominently required online where it is easy to find oneself in an echo-chamber, with one's own particular biases reflected back to them as factual. At a time when problems of 'alternative facts' and 'truthiness' are increasing due to the ease of perpetuating myths through Web 2.0, never is it more crucial to critically assess those claims that *sound* true or are presented as facts, particularly if they pertain to emotionally charged issues. Both critical and compassionate responses are required as and where appropriate in order to understand the morally relevant features of a situation, and in order to decide what to do, how to respond, or whether or not to trust what we are being told. As such, moral agents attend to the particulars of situations, even where they uphold general guidelines, standing propositions, laws or universals. A practical solution to any moral dilemma is going to have to accept that people have gradations of understanding, intelligence, information and even morality, a fact which Kant himself acknowledged (as discussed by Bernard Williams, 1973, in chapter 13). Therefore, an ideal moral rule that is only *possibly* attainable is not as useful as a realistic practical approach which can be applied and used to improve real-life situations.

Critical perspectivism is more encompassing than Nussbaum's ethical mode of attention because it takes into account all perspectives, including technologically conveyed viewpoints which are seemingly un-located (for instance, the Internet and Web 2.0 seem to operate in an omnipresent ether, even though they are connected to specifically located hardware and users). Taking these multiple perspectives into consideration is particularly necessary today in our modern technologically (over-) laden society. Yet there is more room for deception and trickery when the source of our information is mediated via technological tools and sharing platforms that may not have as much transparency as other forms of communication. This is not to say that social media, for instance, cannot be used in a transparent manner. However, media contain various features and constraints that are particular to the tool or platform or app used and a user must be critically engaged with such features and their effects if they are to be discerning. There are more apps, websites, blogs, wikis, forums, discussion boards and social media platforms than one could ever have time to use. The smorgasbord of choice online results in its being too easy to use these tools without reflection or consideration for their impact.

This concern about the potential negative effects of mass art and media has been noted historically by philosophers such as T. W. Adorno and Max Horkheimer (1990). Adorno was specifically concerned about the consumerist society that produces and promotes mass-produced and distributed cultural products which are passively consumed by members of society, creating an insatiable need for ever more 'stuff': information, products, entertainment, the 'new and improved' thing that promises to make a consumer happy. Adorno had a point, even if he had trouble recognising the positive role such mass cultural products could play in society. His worry was an ethical concern about people not pausing to reflect, to think for themselves and question or challenge the perspective they were given on the truth, or on what is valuable, necessary, or pleasurable. The fault lies not in the products or their producers, or the consumers, but in how such products are used, and with what attitude they are received. Adorno's concern was of *passivity*, and a lack of critical engagement. This concern is still relevant today and may be addressed by educating people to be critically perspectival.

Critical perspectivism is necessary in our modern technological world, where many of us have a wealth of resources at our fingertips and a multitude of information constantly 'coming at' us. Not all of the messages heading our way are morally 'good' or accurate. Critical perspectivism (much like other normative moral theories such as utilitarianism and deontological ethics) may sound too intellectually demanding. There is an awful lot of information to attend to, particularly online. The attitude of critical perspectivism is asking us to be more critically engaged with the information we receive, and to pause before unthinkingly basing a decision on what we have been told, or routinely forwarding misinformation or unethical (vicious) messages. This may not be simple, but if we practise this approach, eventually we will be more likely to habituate this critical method of processing information. The tricky part is remaining alert, particularly when social media platforms and the style of conveying news encourage quick responses and flicking through, rather than slowly reading, multiple stories, images and the speedy digestion of bite-sized information. If the subject matter is engaging, we are more likely to be actively critical (as opposed to passive), as the information is being presented in a novel and interesting way. It is precisely for this reason that we may use technological mediums by which to teach critical thinking, for example by exploring different perspectives in a film. Of course Adorno's concern here is noted, that mass forms of entertainment that do not engage the critical thinking skills of viewers may be more dangerous if such (immoral or amoral) messages are passively absorbed by viewers. This idea will be further explored in chapter three.

Critical thinking and adopting many different viewpoints on an issue, integrating this information appropriately, discarding the unnecessary or inaccurate and unhelpful data is the approach taken by one who adopts an attitude of critical perspectivism. When combined with a caring attitude such as that promoted by Nussbaum alongside a virtue ethics framework, critical perspectivism allows us to acknowledge individuals in a context, within a larger social (moral and political) framework.

Minority voices

One thing Nussbaum's loving attitude and critical perspectivism have in common is the desire to seek out, recognise and listen to minority and marginalised voices. An appreciation of and acceptance of diversity does not come at a cost of humanistic ideals and values – on the contrary, accepting difference is often based on recognising that, fundamentally, others are more (not less) like ourselves. Even when it is recognised that some cultural and other minorities are radically different from an existing majority in a particular society at a particular time, there are common human traits that are shared. Moral and other universals do exist and may be shared amongst cultures. Examples of these include moral rules such as 'be kind', 'care for your children', 'avoid harm to yourself and others', and 'do not lie, cheat or steal'. While there may be argument over the interpretation of particular instances or examples of these rules, people still agree that these are important moral rules to uphold. There is also another point against the self-refuting meta-ethical position known as cultural relativism: that there exists just as much diversity within cultural groups as there does between them. The homogenising lens that sees membership of a cultural group as dictating one's values works as a filter that only applies to the majority or powerful voices within that cultural group and misses the fact that there are many sub-cultures within that group. Most ways of dividing people up into categories fails to account for the blurry edges and family resemblances that ensures people often do not neatly fit into one discrete group. Recognising that cultures are not homogenised does not deny the important role a sense of belonging, history, context, culture and the like play in establishing one's sense of personal identity and contributing to feelings of well-being and belonging in communities. Character traits and habits (of expression and value) are indeed shaped by cultural demographics. However, it is also true that we live in a global world, more connected to one another than ever previously and many people are multicultural in either their lineage or displacement or choices. The world is, in many ways, smaller than ever with our ability to move around and connect with others, and neither individual nor cultural variances eradicate the shared human traits we have as people who live a human life. Having said that, it is vital to attend to the various experiences of members of minority groups and particularly of groups that have been historically subjugated and discriminated against. Members of majority groups must work harder than anyone else to employ the compassionate mode of attention that seeks out and engages with stories and perspectives that are different to their own.

Critical perspectivism attempts to respond to Adorno's concern that we are passive receptacles of mass-generated, morally denigrating messages that are symptomatic of the culture of monopoly capitalism of which we are a part and work within. If we unreflectively absorb such mass messages that seek to maintain the status quo and existing discriminations, then we cannot hear different voices when they speak of different experiences, understanding and knowledge. These other voices ought to be expressed and received in a compassionate manner in a safe space lest they be disregarded in favour of the (moral, political and social) majority that holds sway at a particular point in time. Adorno acknowledges that capitalism allows for these different voices to be heard, as each voice has an associated market and consumer group. Yet, even as they are commercialised or mined for their economic value, these voices have a platform from which to be heard. In fact, with the advent of Web 2.0, they have more platforms from which to convey their message than ever previously, able to access a global audience in an instant. Critical perspectivism combats Adorno's concerns by encouraging the employment of a critically engaged and pluralistic attitude, whereby we may be discerning listeners and perceptive viewers who actively and compassionately engage with and critically disseminate the information that surrounds us, upon which we may then act.

This attitude is useful when attending not only to explicit messages that surround us, but also to the implicit messages conveyed via constant media and sources of information that are a constant presence in our environment. I believe it is actually these implicit messages with which Adorno was concerned. An example of how critical perspectivism is useful is demonstrable when children or adults are faced with the broadcasted news. The news has become filmic in its presentation, playing like a blockbuster film with streaming headlines, cut-shots and hyped-up newsworthy events. How can one discern between differing levels of threat when everything is so very important? Our society's obsession with Reality TV, gossip and drama may explain why we have entered a post-truth age where the emotions and sensations evoked matter more than the facts. Our current age is fast becoming one in which larger than life, egoistical personalities count for more than intelligence or wisdom, an age in which we seek to be entertained rather than informed. This appetite for infotainment and excessive emotional displays seems further propelled by Web 2.0 and the advent of social media, which feeds our constant cravings. Operating within a 24-hour news cycle full of click bait headlines in a global marketplace, we have instant access to stories of all kinds at all times. Challenging the sources and asking questions is vital if we are to ascertain the level to which we are affected by such messages.

Questions that are asked of media should include who is the assumed viewer and what morals are being conveyed and what voices are being left out or trivialised as well as which voices are being included as conveying facts when they are actually representing subjective opinion. Children, as vulnerable members of the audience, must also be taught to be savvy in similar ways, particularly when faced with 'information overload' that is common in our fast-paced technological world. Parents and teachers, who often take the role of assisting children to decipher such news programmes, will be better at teaching children the critical analytical skills required if they themselves are using such skills. Thus the skills of the critical thinker are necessary to enable a person to distinguish between fact and fiction, whole-truths or embellishment. In a post-truth age, this is of more importance than ever before. Such thinking skills may be taught and are transferable to everyday life, allowing critical thinkers to apply such techniques to the messages gained from, for instance, the news or social media. We collect information, news and infotainment daily from numerous sources. Because of this, we require the ability to sift through these facts (or 'alternative facts') in order to construct a 'bigger picture'; higher-order thinkers can see and analyse the frameworks upon which such pieces of information rest and thereby discern what is truthful as opposed to what is simply false, gossip, rumour or propaganda.

One way the critical thinking skills of logical analysis, reasonable deliberation, intellectual discernment and ethical deliberation may be taught and practised is through the teaching of philosophy in schools and by well-facilitated communities of inquiry. As will be further argued for in chapter five, these pedagogical techniques encourage critical and creative thinking alongside a caring attitude. Many educational studies show that this method works remarkably well with demonstrated results in terms of children's improved lateral thinking, logical deduction, higher-order thinking and behaviour, including evidence of increased tolerance and less bullying in the school yard. Collaborative learning is effectively proven in educational studies to increase learning, retention, understanding and thus knowledge. A caring attitude allows different viewpoints to be expressed and heard. Ideally, students will progress from a relativistic and uncritical or unreflective opinion to an informed stance that bases belief on evidence and respects the role one plays in a larger community of inquirers who evaluate and assess ideas. This is the basis for real compromise and understanding. This is the goal of adopting the attitude I have called critical perspectivism.

Conclusion

We live in a global community and, as such, we have a need to empathise with others from diverse backgrounds with different cultural, socio-political and religious views that inform at least the expression of values, if not values themselves. Establishing our moral character by practising the virtues and ethical attention, while honing our critical thinking skills is an aim to which educators aspire. As a mode of being critically as well as compassionately engaged in the world, critical perspectivism is an attitude that allows moral agents to discern the epistemic and moral value of the multiple texts, images and narratives that are unavoidable in our daily lives. In this way, critical perspectivism encourages an independent mind that collaborates with others and finds what is best for all. One who adopts a critically perspectival attitude will hold all answers or perspectives together, examining each, critically as well as sympathetically. In this way, an ethical agent may critique and empathetically attend to the facts of a situation in order to rationally deduce what is the right thing to do.

Critical perspectivism is not 'cold' or inhumane; it allows for the pluralism that exists in life that we must take into account when dealing with moral dilemmas and adds the critical component required for reflection upon the differing viewpoints with which we are faced. In this contemporary sense, critical perspectivism is most effective in the modern world of multiple information sources, as it provides a mode by which we can gather and discern between what we are told, the various sources of such information, and assimilate and apply that which is relevant with regard to its practical application and purpose.

As a moral attitude, critical perspectivism offers us a manner of critiquing the multiple sources of information that are forcibly directed our way. As technology increases the rate and amount of information we receive, we must seek to morally evaluate and assimilate useful information, while discarding misinformation and avoiding hoaxes and scams. We also need to keep in mind that others with whom we agree or disagree, play games or live chat are also thinking and feeling human beings hidden behind an avatar or online profile. Bearing these things in mind will assist us to seek truth and treat others ethically, even while protecting ourselves from various threats or commonplace misinformation. We must firstly see and defend the value in seeking truth and treating others in an ethical manner and note that, even while such values are universal, not everyone will be considerate or compassionate. Critical perspectivism has two central features: it is compassionate and it is critical. In chapters two and three, I will examine each of these features further in turn, considering the role they play in our responses to people and mediated information, with the aim of seeking knowledge, wisdom and ethical relationships.

References

Adorno, T. W., & Horkheimer, M. (1990). The culture industry: Enlightenment as mass deception. In T. W. Adorno & M. Horkheimer (Eds.), *Dialectic of enlightenment*. New York: Continuum and also Adorno, T. W. (1991). *The culture industry: Selected essays on mass culture* (J. M. Bernstein, Ed.). London: Routledge.

Ciprian, M. (2015). *The role of ethical theories in the decision making of Australian animal ethics committees: a multi-method examination*. Unpublished PhD Dissertation. The University of Western Australia. Scholar's Centre. Accessible via UWA Research Repository. Retrieved from http://research-repository.uwa.edu.au/

D'Olimpio, L., & Teschers, C. (2017). Playing with philosophy: Gestures, performance, P4C and an art of living. *Educational Philosophy and Theory*, Special Issue 'Aesthetic Education' Ed. Elizabeth Grierson. Retrieved from http://www.tandfonline.com/doi/abs/10.1080/00131857.2017.1294974

Hand, M. (2014). Towards a theory of moral education. *Journal of Philosophy of Education, 48*(4), 519–532.

Kant, I. (1983). *Metaphysical principles of virtue* (J. W. Ellington, trans.). Indianapolis: Hackett.

MacIntyre, A. (2008). *After virtue*. Notre Dame, IN: University of Notre Dame Press.

Marcuse, H. (1965/1969). Repressive tolerance. In R. P. Wolff, B. Moore, Jr., & H. Marcuse (Eds.), *A critique of pure tolerance*. Boston: Beacon Press.

Murdoch, I. (1970). *The sovereignty of good*. Boston: Routledge & Kegan Paul.

Nietzsche, F. (1872). *The birth of tragedy* (C. P. Fadiman, trans.). New York: Dover.

Nietzsche, F. (1974/1882). *The gay science* (W. Kaufmann, trans.). New York: Vintage Books.

Nietzsche, F. (1994/1887). *On the genealogy of morality* (K. Ansell-Pearson, Ed., & C. Diethe, trans.). Cambridge: Cambridge University Press.

Nussbaum, M. C. (1990). *Love's knowledge*. Oxford: Oxford University Press.

Nussbaum, M. C. (1995). *Poetic justice: The literary imagination and public life*. Boston: Beacon Press.

Nussbaum, M. (1998). The Transfigurations of Intoxication: Nietzsche, Schopenhauer and Dionysus, in *Nietzsche, Philosophy and the Arts*, by Kemal, Gaskell and Conway (Eds). Cambridge: Cambridge University Press.

Nussbaum, M. C. (2000). *Women and human development: The capabilities approach*. Cambridge: Cambridge University Press.

Nussbaum, M. C. (2001). *Upheavals of thought: The intelligence of emotions*. Cambridge: Cambridge University Press.

Noddings, N. (1984). *Caring: A feminine approach to ethics and moral education*. Berkeley: University of California Press.

Richardson, H. S. (1998). Nussbaum: Love and respect. *Metaphilosophy, 24*(9), 254–262.

Swanton, C. (2003). *Virtue ethics: A pluralistic view*. Oxford: Oxford University Press.

Swanton, C. (2015). *The virtue ethics of Hume and Nietzsche*. Oxford: John Wiley & Sons.

Weil, S. (1978). *Lectures on philosophy*. Cambridge: Cambridge University Press.

Williams, B. (1973). *Problems of the self*. Cambridge: Cambridge University Press.

2   Compassionate engagement

Critical perspectivism is an attitude that supports a practise of being morally engaged in the world by processing and understanding information received from mass-produced and distributed media sources in a critical and compassionate manner. A moral agent who is critically perspectival will be critical of what they read, see and hear, while also being appropriately compassionate towards others they encounter. These others may be encountered face-to-face or online in a virtual space, and critical perspectivism may be adopted in various scenarios. Importantly, when one interacts with others, particularly with others with whom one disagrees, a moral attitude involves recognising that the people with whom one interacts are much like oneself and capable of suffering or being harmed in particular ways. With this in mind, the caring aspect of critical perspectivism is highlighted as vital if we are to treat others with respect. This does not mean we must agree with everything another says so as not to hurt their feelings, but we should be mindful of the way we communicate with others when conveying, receiving, and processing information. Where appropriate, we ought to feel and demonstrate compassionate regard for others.

Compassion is best understood as a virtue that comprises particular emotional, cognitive and active responses which recognise a shared and common humanity. If we are compassionate, we are able to put ourselves in the shoes of another and consider what they may need. Importantly, if we feel compassionate concern towards that person, we may also then be motivated to act in a way that may help. As critical perspectivism asks that moral agents adopt a compassionate as well as a critical attitude, we may well ask what kind of compassionate response is being called for and to whom should such compassion be directed. In this chapter, I will explore the answers to these questions, while also making the case that compassion is a *good* or ethical response, when properly and appropriately directed.

If I am successful in providing compelling reasons to believe that we should indeed be compassionate, then the next question of interest is how we may educate people to be ethically engaged in this way. Can we teach people to be compassionate, or is compassion an innate trait rather than a habituated response? There must be care taken to try to untangle compassion from related emotions such as sympathy and empathy, even while recognising the family resemblances that connect them. Empathy (feeling the feelings of another or, more specifically, imaginatively reconstructing the feelings of another), or sympathy (feeling *for* another or identifying with the other based on feelings of common humanity), assists us to feel compassionate concern for others who are suffering. However, I defend compassion as more rational and useful for a flourishing life than either empathy or sympathy because it involves a certain amount of critical distance from the other who suffers. This is why compassion has a role to play in critical perspectivism.

Martha Nussbaum defends compassion as a moral response that may be cultivated through imaginative engagement with aesthetically and ethically good works of narrative art. Narrative art includes works of literature and film. If we engage in a sympathetic manner with the characters and scenarios depicted within narrative artworks, we may practise a 'loving attitude' or caring disposition that is useful in application to the real world. Upon this virtue ethics framework, practising such a compassionate disposition may eventually result in this moral and rational habit becoming habituated and, over time, engrained in our character. I shall critically examine Nussbaum's claims and then, in chapter three, consider how this relates to other forms of mass media, including social media and online information sources.

Why compassion?

Along with virtue ethics, compassion is enjoying a renaissance in popularity within the fields of moral philosophy, psychology and education. The emphasis on compassion as a form of care in the caring professions is widely recognised and understood. Vocations such as nursing, medicine and teaching incorporate the idea that nurses, doctors and teachers should display care as one of the duties contained within their professional ethics and codes of conduct. Expanding upon this, caring about others just seems like a *nice thing to do*, and, following the Golden Rule, one would generally like others to care about them. It is important to question this assumption, of course, and investigate how caring about others can help them (as well as oneself) to flourish. Importantly, one will feel compassion towards another only if they firstly recognise that the other is a fellow human being much like themselves. Also importantly, it is worth noting that if a moral agent should care about others, then they should also care about themselves.

Yet we may also rightly be wary of some seemingly caring emotions such as empathy or pity or sympathy. Of some cause for concern is the subjective and partial nature of such responses. Emotions, after all, are tricky things and are not always (or not even sometimes) reasonable, impartial, consistent or rational. This makes them more difficult for moral purposes if we are seeking to make normative claims with respect to the ethical responses moral agents should have in particular situations towards certain people. Some people are simply not very sympathetic, and others may be sympathetic only to their family and friends or people they like (who, presumably, like them too). Conversely, some people are nicer to strangers than they are to those closest to them! If compassion is to be defended as a moral response, is it unfair to be partial with respect to whom we feel compassion? And, on the other end of the scale, we may ask if there is such a thing as being too sympathetic, let alone whether it really is desirable or even possible to feel a universal form of care (or compassion or *agape*) towards every single human being or living creature.

In the wake of the global refugee crisis and the looming threat of climate change, world leaders, including political and religious leaders, celebrities and activists have often called upon humanity to respond to such ethical issues with compassion. If we take seriously the Aristotelian starting premise that human beings are social, moral and political creatures, we realise that we share the world and, in this way, are global citizens. For instance, the impending threat of the effects of climate change make it such that we are all accountable for how we protect the earth's resources for the sake of future generations. While we may make a moral argument for ethical action on the basis of utility, overall good, or standing principles and obligations, we may also recognise that a rational emotion such as compassion may appropriately accompany and motivate moral action. When we take the point of view of others, even future others, in order to consider what a flourishing life should entail – not just for myself and my family, but for all – we are more likely to feel and act upon compassion and care in an effort to *do the right thing*.

Andrew Peterson (2016) identifies two characteristics of compassion that make it uniquely qualified to support the development of moral dispositions:

> compassion requires some form of harmony between sympathy (the care-based sorrow we feel at the suffering of others) and empathy (the 'imaginative reconstruction', to use Blum's (1987, p. 232) term of the others' suffering, which blends self- and other-focused role-taking; for a fuller discussion of these elements of compassion, see Peterson, 2016). Once these two characteristics of compassion are identified, the realisation that one's imaginative reconstruction of an other (in compassion's case an other who is suffering) may be fallible becomes crucial, and moves the compassionate subject to engage further in order to understand the other. Such understanding forms a crucial part in the discernment and deliberation central to *phronesis* (or practical wisdom).
>
> (D'Olimpio & Peterson, 2017)

If compassion can help us to be prudent by helping us to discern the morally relevant features of a situation, then it may be useful when we are trying to judge what the ethical response looks like in practical terms. To this end, compassion is a good habit to cultivate. Yet it can be difficult to feel compassion towards others when one is caught up in one's own life, with one's own concerns, projects and activities occupying our central focus. Compassion requires time and effort to exert – it involves pausing to think about how another might be affected. It is certainly not always, or even often, easy to be compassionate. If we are seeking to train compassion as a habitual response, it may be that we can learn and practise this moral attitude by engaging with the stories of others' lives, whether these be real or fictional.

Learning from narrative artworks

Using narratives, whether texts or personal stories, is a common way to teach values, especially to young children. Narratives engage our emotions, as well as our rational intellect, and are more likely to motivate action than an abstract theory. Starting from the Aristotelian assumption that human beings are storytelling animals, Nussbaum claims that we can learn, (morally) from narrative artworks. She argues that we can, through imaginative and sympathetic engagement with the stories of diverse others, learn to adopt a moral attitude. We can practise this caring disposition when hearing about the experiences of others, even if, and sometimes even more so when, these others are fictional characters. In this way, some (aesthetically and ethically good) narrative artworks may have a morally educative role to play.

While Nussbaum's argument applies to novels, and the examples she gives are particularly of realist and/or classical works, she does not preclude film from the category of 'narrative art', thereby allowing some mass artworks to be morally educative (Nussbaum, 1995, p. 6). Nussbaum compares how literary works and works of moral philosophy may both be committed to truth-telling and to representing ideas using language. She is careful to point out that her argument does not apply to *all* works of art, or all narrative artworks. Nussbaum notes:

> One can think of works of art which can be contemplated reasonably well without asking any urgent questions about how one should live. Abstract formalist paintings are sometimes of this character, and some intricate but non-programmatic works of music (though by no means all). But it seems highly unlikely that a responsive reading of any complex literary work is utterly detached from concerns about time and death, about pain and the transcendence of pain, and so on – all the material of 'how one should live' questions as I have conceived it.
>
> (Nussbaum, 1998, p. 358)

And it is questions about how we should live that are of interest in the moral realm. In attempting to address this question of what we should do and of what a good life consists, both rational argumentation in an academic style and some works of literature may be morally educative. Yet good (aesthetically and ethically) works of literature may be more persuasive and accessible to a wider audience precisely because of the narrative style employed by the writers. Nussbaum claims that "Plato" (works of moral philosophy) and "Proust" (literature) "both share a certain vague conception of their task or aim. They view themselves as using speech in order to tell truth about the human soul to human souls. But they clearly have enormously different ways of engaging the reader in the search for truth" (Nussbaum, 1990, p. 258). Obviously the literary artworks are going to be read by a larger number of people than treatises on moral philosophy. Films and television shows will be even more popular, and the ease of access as a result of current technology points to their significance in society if they indeed may have a positive, or detrimental, effect on viewers.

Yet the kind of effect stories can have is difficult to quantify or articulate in any more than a correlative manner. The causal impact of stories must be subjective and contextual, yet it seems reasonable that the engaging nature of storytelling is something that appeals to human psychology. Stories and images can activate emotions and stimulate ideas which can, in turn, motivate action. Furthermore, narrative artworks may be understood by people of varying education and age levels and, in this way, are much more inclusive than, say, a technical work of moral philosophy published in a journal that may be accessed only by those with subscriptions or appropriate institutional affiliations.

One way we can learn, morally, from fictions, is by practising a 'loving attitude' or caring disposition towards characters and the scenarios in which they find themselves. By practising this moral attitude in relation to characters in stories, we are protected in a safe fictional space, which makes it easier to try to imaginatively engage with other perspectives:

> The aesthetic activity, which takes place in a safe and protected 'potential space' where our own safety is not immediately threatened, harnesses the pleasure of exploring to the neediness and insufficiency that is its object, thus making our limitations pleasing, and at least somewhat less threatening, to ourselves.
>
> (Nussbaum, 2001, p. 244)

Practising compassionate responses to people and situations may occur daily when we encounter others and hear the stories they tell about their lives and their experiences. Yet we can also practise compassion by imaginatively engaging with fictional stories that convey different perspectives and experiences – even some that we may never encounter in our own lives. Protected in the fictional world, I can safely explore various storylines, including considering characters' intentions, actions and the resulting effects in my mind's eye.

For example, I can learn what it is like for Huckleberry Finn in Missouri in the 1800s, even if slavery has not been legal in my lifetime. Furthermore, even if I haven't visited America, I can learn more about racism by reading this book and apply the universal themes to the time and place in which I live, because of the way Mark Twain has depicted the events and characters. I can reflect on the ethical concepts and consider how they still apply today. By putting myself in the shoes of Huck and Jim, I can feel compassion towards the characters and the situation they find themselves in, even while knowing that this is a work of fiction. We can learn from fictions in this way because human experiences are universal.

This account of moral education goes beyond learning to strictly adhere to moral rules and thus allows for or encourages, or perhaps even necessitates, the moral training and habituation of relevant rational emotions. While we may want people to simply follow the rules and 'do no harm', it is the definition, application and manifestation of these rules that are important in society. For instance, Nussbaum argues that respect "is blind unless the "inner eyes" are cultivated. . . . But principles do not apply themselves: we first must have appropriate perceptions of the salient features of the situation before us" (Nussbaum, 2012, p. 143). In the example of Huckleberry Finn, we see that it is important not to blindly follow laws or social norms that are unethical. Rather, moral agents who are critical and compassionate will feel a sense of tension because their experiences are not conforming to what is expected by society at the time. It is the attention to ethically relevant features of a situation that helps us to make good moral decisions, by knowing which details to take into account when we are trying to work out what we should do. And this moral attentiveness requires practical wisdom, which must be practised. As Nussbaum is a self-proclaimed neo-Aristotelian, virtue ethics can provide us with a useful framework by which to understand the epistemological and ethical concepts being employed here.

In order to develop moral character, we must learn and then practise the virtues until they are automatic habits and become incorporated into our character. Aristotle defines the virtues as mid-point between excessive and deficient behaviour; for instance, courage is a virtue, and fear (which is deficient) and rashness (which is excessive) are vices. Following the doctrine of the mean, we aim for what is appropriate in a given situation, after rationally taking into account our personal capabilities. Virtuous actions are supported by good intentions and appropriate emotional dispositions. For example, we would call someone *compassionate* only if they are habitually compassionate, and act in this way because they think it's the appropriate moral response. In this way, the virtues must be supported by the intellectual virtue of *phronesis* or practical wisdom. On this account, it is not enough to know the right thing to do; we also need to understand the right way to do it ('knowing how' must accompany 'knowing that').

The virtues assist individuals to live a flourishing life, or a life of *eudaimonia*, because we are social creatures whose behaviour impacts upon those around us. Therefore, character traits occupy a central position on an Aristotelian account of the good life. We learn the virtues (or vices) from a young age as we practise actions that become habits which are influenced by our environment and upbringing, our peers and role models. A person's character is developed according to their habitual actions, and Aristotle (*NE*, Book 11, Chapter 1) explains that the virtues arise in us neither according to nature nor contrary to nature, but nature gives us the capacity to acquire the virtues, and they are attained only via habituation. This account relies on a cognitive understanding of the emotions as "feelings can be properly thoughtful, just as thoughts can be properly felt" (Kristjansson, 2007, p. 18). So the question arises as to which habits or virtues we should promote and how we can practise these whilst avoiding vices. For Nussbaum, the virtue of compassion, a rational emotion, is one such habit we should practise until we reflexively adopt a caring attitude towards others and the environment. One way we can encourage, practise and develop the virtue of compassion is by engaging with aesthetically and ethically good narrative artworks.

Moral knowledge

If we are to practise compassionate responses towards fictions, the narratives in question must be, in an important sense, realistic. Certainly, narratives must be somewhat like our own world and experiences in order for us to identify with, understand and interpret them correctly; if novels weren't at all based in reality they wouldn't make any sense. Nussbaum claims that literary artworks are not only life-like enough, but they also best capture the subtleties of real moral dilemmas and thus provide us with a useful proxy in order to practise moral discernment. This is evident as novels often make use of linear time; the characters are humans with thoughts, emotions and who act upon a world in a similar way to us. Even science fiction stories have enough similarities to make them relevant and meaningful to their readers. Nussbaum argues that, if we meaningfully engage with, and practise an ethical mode of attention to scenarios and characters depicted, this can enable us to learn, among other things, general moral truths.

Moral knowledge on this account is wider than that of a solely propositional account. Here Nussbaum draws upon the pragmatist and author Henry James, claiming that moral knowledge restricted to propositions would be incomplete, and what is needed is a broader understanding. On this account, "[m]oral knowledge . . . is not simply intellectual grasp of propositions; it is not even simply intellectual grasp of particular facts; it is perception. It is seeing a complex, concrete reality in a highly lucid and richly responsive way; it is taking in what is there, with imagination and feeling" (Nussbaum, 1990 p. 152). In illustrating her point, Nussbaum analyses Henry James's *A Golden Bowl*. James's work is considered as an example of (perhaps rare) narrative art that is both aesthetically and ethically good. The intricate detail with which James describes the characters, their inner worlds, as well as their moral dilemmas is what particularly resonates with the attentive reader. Nussbaum claims that "this prose itself displays a view of moral attention", and, furthermore, "the text itself displays, and is, a high kind of moral activity" (1990, p. 161). This is a big claim, to call the artwork itself an example of moral activity. Nussbaum argues that the attentive and sympathetic reader will be practising a moral attitude when engaging with such a text because such a reader will actively care about and participate in the story. Such a novel, "calls forth our "active sense of life", which is our moral faculty" (Nussbaum, 1990, p. 162).

If this is true, then creating such artworks, as well as engaging with them, is not an 'easy' or passive process. One feature of such engagement is that the artist and the person receiving the artwork is committed to truth seeking. Nussbaum is here inspired by Iris Murdoch, who defends the artist's responsibility to truth-telling within their medium, claiming that in art:

> we are presented with a truthful image of the human condition in a form which can be steadily contemplated, and indeed this is the only context in which many of us are capable of contemplating it at all. Art transcends selfish and obsessive limitations of personality and can enlarge the sensibility of its consumer.
>
> (Murdoch, 1970, p. 84)

It is this truthful depiction that allows the viewer to imaginatively and unselfishly engage with another's perspective, a practise which can assist us in our moral judgements. According to Murdoch, this ethical mode of attention requires bravery and an unselfishness whereby we can look for the value in ideas that differ from our own. The artist, who creates the aesthetically and ethically good novel or film, must also produce their artwork in this same manner – a difficult task to be sure, and many mass-produced and distributed artworks will certainly fall short.

Murdoch defends a disinterested and unselfish form of attention that viewers should use when engaging with artworks, as well as when making moral decisions, or considering others. This ethical perspective is also loving, and inclines one towards others. Murdoch notes, "I have used the word 'attention', which I borrow from Simone Weil, to express the idea of a just and loving gaze directed upon an individual reality. I believe this to be the characteristic and proper mark of the active moral agent" (Murdoch, 1970, p. 33). There is the idea that a moral person will be just and loving, and it is this form of steady contemplation that reveals things, and people, 'as they really are' (Murdoch, 1970, p. 36). Now, this seems to be a perfect form of ethical attention to which we should aspire, rather than an everyday way of seeing and responding to people and situations, and I say this because Murdoch speaks of this 'patient, loving regard' as being usual for saints, and artists (Murdoch, 1970, p. 39). Why Murdoch elevates the artist to this great lofty height is uncertain, although, surely, great art can indeed inspire an ethical mode of attention in its viewers, offering us a different perspective, and artworks may accomplish this even when the artists are not themselves perfectly ethical beings.

Focussing on the audience reception of artworks, Nussbaum offers a positive causal link between morality and literature, as she believes that *good* literature can assist us in understanding morality. In this way, literature may enable attentive and sympathetic readers to practise virtuous conduct, which may positively inform our ethical decision making in our everyday lives. This causal connection between the work of literature and the moral agent's caring attitude towards others is predicated on the idea that, by practising a loving attitude towards characters in works of fiction, we care about their plight. Nussbaum claims that, "by identifying with them and allowing ourselves to be surprised (an attitude of mind that storytelling fosters and develops), we become more responsive to our own life's adventure, more willing to see and be touched by life" (1990, p. 162). If we practise this moral attitude first in the safe fictional space, we can then apply it to real-life others we encounter. Attentive readers can find themselves more attuned to moral nuances in their everyday lives as they are involved in a "friendly participation in the adventures of the concrete characters, but also an attempt to see the novel as a paradigm of something that might happen in his or her own life" (Nussbaum, 1990, p. 166).

This causal argument will work only if we see humans as rational and emotional, embodied and situated in a social and political context. Both Murdoch and Nussbaum's 'loving attitude' or form of ethical attention requires a certain amount of objectivity or 'justice' alongside a concern for others. This loving attitude calls on the love or compassion (a feeling component with a cognitive element as well as a volitional aspect) working alongside the intellect and the imagination. These three elements work together in order to understand the facts of a particular situation, whereby the ethical agent may feel care for an other, usually an other who is suffering, by imaginatively engaging with their plight and then 'seeing' how to appropriately respond. This occurs in real life as well as when imaginatively engaging with narrative artworks. The imagination, emotions and narratives – stories, then – are important to a holistic approach to being human. Nussbaum explains:

> I defend the literary imagination precisely because it seems to me an essential ingredient of an ethical stance that asks us to concern ourselves with the good of other people whose lives are distant from our own. . . . [A]n ethics of impartial respect for human dignity will fail to engage real human beings unless they are capable of entering imaginatively into the lives of distant others and to have emotions related to that participation.
>
> (Nussbaum, 1995, xvi)

If we attempt to engage with a notion expressed as black-and-white, cold, hard facts, we may miss vital aspects such as the motivation, intention and comprehension of the agent involved. It is for these reasons that Nussbaum claims that, because of their ability to flesh out complex scenarios and depict characters with nuanced personalities, narrative artworks are a better text to learn from when it comes to moral education. In this way, narratives are better than dry, logical texts usually written by moral philosophers that depict their arguments about moral principles as abstract rules, divorced from the realities of everyday life.

Thus, due to their complexity and nuance, narrative artworks are realistic, despite the fact that they are works of fiction. Given stories are told using language, they also express moral values. According to Murdoch, judgements about value(s) are unavoidable in narrative works, as "one cannot avoid value judgements. Values show, and show clearly, in literature" (Murdoch quoted in Magee, 1978, p. 278). Value judgements are imbedded in our language and the words we use often imply or presume certain kinds of moral evaluations. Murdoch notes that:

> It is important to remember that language itself is a moral medium, almost all uses of language convey value. This is one reason why we are almost always morally active. Life is soaked in the moral, literature is soaked in the moral . . . So the novelist is revealing his values by any sort of writing which he may do. He is particularly bound to make moral judgements in so far as his subject-matter is the behaviour of human beings.
>
> (Murdoch, 1998, pp. 27–28)

An example of how morally loaded our language is can be seen when we ask questions that contain ethical considerations. When I ask a question, I reveal my bias, assumptions and values. For instance, asking the question 'What should be done about climate change?' reveals a very different ethical starting point and assumption from the question 'Is climate change real?' Writers, as social, moral agents, are always deliberately selecting their words and the expression used by characters in their stories. These choices will reveal values, assumptions and biases, just as do those chosen (or unthinkingly, habitually used, or blurted out) in everyday life. Writers often make such selections with a purpose in mind, and this purpose may include a desire to represent a character's values as open to critique or condemnation.

In this way, fictional stories may explore morality and convey general moral truths in much the same way as lived human experience. In fact, it is this common humanity that allows us to engage with and respond to artworks and be able to find such works meaningful. It is also what allows us to sympathetically attend to, and learn from, the characters and scenarios depicted in narrative artworks. As Nussbaum remarks, the arts and the humanities work to activate and expand our capacity 'to see the world through another person's eyes' (Nussbaum, 2010, p. 96). This correlation between the narrative artwork, the reader's imagination and a moral agent's feeling of compassion towards others who suffer links the story to moral activity whereby the emotionally engaged reader feels a relevant sense of care for others.

Aesthetics and ethics

This inclination to make ethical judgements of aesthetic works is not an altogether popular position amongst aestheticians or artists, many of whom are Formalists. Autonomism, also known as "aestheticism", states that art and ethics are autonomous realms of value. Autonomists argue that the only relevant evaluation of an artwork is that of the aesthetic, as it is only an artistic focus that is relevant *qua* work of art. Radical autonomism, such as the position held by Clive Bell from the Bloomsbury Group, states that it doesn't even make sense to assess a work of art in terms of morality (or politics or cognition) (Young, 2005, p. 70). The position of the radical autonomist has evolved as a theoretical argument whereby the very definition of aesthetic evaluation is based on the exclusion of moral evaluation of an art object. Designed to protect the autonomy of aesthetic value, and prohibit censorship of artists, the position of the radical autonomist lacks practical application by prohibiting any ethical evaluation or comments on artworks. The position known as moderate autonomism allows for a moral assessment to be made, yet argues that the work's moral value does not affect the aesthetic value or overall value of the artwork.

Against this view, the moderate moralist or the ethicist will defend the ethical evaluation that can be made of artworks. These theorists thus allow art objects to convey moral values, have a moral effect and be thusly critiqued. Moderate moralism holds that some works are concerned with morality and, in such cases, moral evaluation is relevant and may impact upon the work's overall aesthetic value, whereas the ethicist defends an 'all-things-considered' judgement to be made with respect to artworks. I support the adoption of an 'all-things-considered' judgement, although the position of moderate moralism equally serves my purposes. Artworks can and should be evaluated based on their formal features, as well as their ethical component, which may very well comprise an aspect of their formal features. This may be seen where a novel invites sympathy to an underserving character. The prescribed audience response may be unable to be adopted by a moral agent reading the story precisely because the character is immoral. If asked to sympathise with this character, the prevention of the uptake of the prescribed response is a formal flaw in the work as well as an ethical flaw (Carroll, 2000, p. 15).

It is the case that autonomists are trying to protect the unique and intrinsic value of art objects, yet to ignore the instrumental or moral aspects of art ignores the fact that art objects are created by human beings, who are also moral agents, in the world. Aesthetes or Formalists who claim that an artwork ought to be judged on its own merit without reference to any external or authorial features argue that the aesthetic (and overall) value of an artwork is based solely on aesthetic (formal) components of that work. Formalists and autonomists regard the aesthetic experience as "the experience prescribed by an artwork that is valued for its own sake (and not for the sake of anything else, including moral enlightenment or moral improvement)" (Carroll, 2000, p. 3). Yet often artists are making moral claims and encouraging a critical response to worldly issues through their art and this is an extremely valuable practice.

Take, for example, the author Oscar Wilde and his novels, which are famous for challenging the social mores of his time. I claim that, despite his explicit comments, it is absolutely false that Oscar Wilde was an aestheticist. Wilde is known for arguing that there is no such thing as a good or bad book; rather, books are well or badly written and that is all (Wilde, 1891, *preface*). Yet Wilde's books contain moral messages that are almost impossible for the reader to ignore, and he took the line of the aesthete in order to publish such sentiments and avoid censorship or rebuke (which was unsuccessful in his case). It can be argued that Wilde is actually an ethicist, as his works are completely concerned with the ethical in such a way that makes it impossible to suppose that the values of art and morality can be divorced. It is the moral message of *Dorian Gray* that largely contributed to making it a great work, and Wilde knew this to be the case. Yet it is a separate, albeit related issue as to whether we can learn morally from reading aesthetically and ethically good narrative artworks such as the works of Oscar Wilde or Henry James.

Indeed, one aesthetician who argues against Nussbaum's claim that we can learn moral truths from literary artworks is Richard Posner. Posner holds that we cannot ethically critique artworks and his disagreement with Nussbaum is further based on his narrower view of the kinds of moral features a work of art can hope to contain or transmit. Posner is particularly sceptical of the causal claim that certain literature can help develop its readers' moral abilities.

In her response to Posner, Nussbaum clarifies the claims she is making, stating:

> Posner's attack is directed at two very different works: *Love's Knowledge*, where my primary concern is with moral philosophy, and with the claim that moral philosophy needs certain carefully selected works of narrative literature

in order to pursue its own task in a complete way; and *Poetic Justice*, where my concern is with the conduct of public deliberations in democracy, and where my claim is that literature of a carefully specified sort can offer valuable assistance to such deliberations by both cultivating and reinforcing valuable moral abilities. In neither work do I make any general claims about 'literature' as such; indeed, I explicitly eschew such claims in both works, and I insist that my argument is confined to a narrow group of pre-selected works.

(Nussbaum, 1998, p. 346)

But if you thought this weakened Nussbaum's claim linking aesthetics and ethics, you would be mistaken. She contends that "certain novels are, irreplaceably, works of moral philosophy. But I shall go further . . . the novel can be a paradigm of moral activity" (Nussbaum, 1990, p. 148).

Posner objects, citing instances of literature-loving Nazis and English professors who are no more moral than anyone else (Posner, 1997, pp. 4–5), while also reminding us of the importance of a good upbringing when it comes to moral formation. However, Nussbaum needn't deny these examples in order to still defend her position. In fact, she happily grants Posner's point that empathy or sympathy or compassion in and of itself will not sufficiently motivate good action, and such an emotion must be grounded in a good early education in childhood for it to motivate any moral concern for others (Nussbaum, 1998, p. 352). Nussbaum simply claims that some literature *can* have a morally beneficial effect, not that it always will. However, for those instances where a good narrative artwork does have such an effect, the reading of that work itself can be deemed a moral act. It is worth noting, though, for the aesthetically and ethically good artwork to have such an effect, the reader themselves must be appropriately sensitive and adopt a loving attitude in order to engage compassionately with the characters and scenario depicted.

Adopting a caring disposition towards fictional stories may seem like a nice thing to do, but how does that result in moral truth? Does it not simply confirm moral truths the reader already knows? This argument from cognitive triviality is detailed nicely by Nöel Carroll as follows:

> Suppose that [Käthe] Kollwitz's Municipal Lodging is taken to reveal that. the poor are oppressed. That hardly counts as a moral discovery; it was surely well known before the picture was made. In fact, it makes little sense to say that the picture "revealed" this truism. Rather, the painting appears to presuppose it. That is, the painting requires viewers already in possession of this viewpoint in order to recognise its articulation in the picture and to be moved to indignation by it.
>
> (Carroll, 2000, p. 3)

Carroll then goes on to defend Nussbaum's thesis, calling it an example of a 'cultivation approach', in terms of elucidating the kind of moral education that may be occurring when we morally engage with appropriate novels. Labelling the position Posner inhabits as that of the sceptic, Carroll explains that "the skeptic's conception of education is too narrow":

> For the skeptic, education is the acquisition of insightful propositions about the moral life. For the advocate of the cultivation approach, education may also involve other things, including the honing of ethically relevant skills and powers (such as the capacity for finer perceptual discrimination, the imagination, the emotions, and the overall ability to conduct moral reflection) as well as the exercise and refinement of moral understanding (that is, the improvement and sometimes the expansion of our understanding of the moral precepts and concepts we already possess). As the label for this approach indicates, the educative value of art resides in its potential to cultivate our moral talents.
>
> (Carroll, 2000, p. 367)

Propositional moral truths, or *knowing that*, may not be the kind of truths we are learning through our engagement with literature. About this, Posner or the sceptic may indeed be correct. However, drawing upon Gilbert Ryle's distinction between *knowing that* and *knowing how*, we may be learning about the contextual application of morality or 'what it is like' via imaginatively adopting other perspectives and thinking through various scenarios in our minds. This *knowing how* or '*knowing what it is like*' is a pragmatic aspect of moral knowledge (Hepburn, 1990). I may, for instance, know that I would not like to go to jail, as this would be an unpleasant experience and this knowledge may suffice to prevent me from committing criminal acts. I may further augment this propositional knowledge with a vicarious experience of what it might be like to be in jail. If I have never been incarcerated and if I do not know anyone who has ever served time, I might learn what it is like by reading Dostoyevsky's *The Brothers Karamazov* or by watching Netflix's television series *Orange Is the New Black* (created by Jenji Kohan). Carroll rightly includes 'knowing what it is like' as a part of 'knowing how' and this kind of knowledge that we can learn from fictions is sufficient to defeat Posner and the argument from cognitive triviality.

Caring and critical

The 'care' that Nussbaum speaks of is a mode of sympathetic ethical attention that one can pay to others in order to try to understand their plight, particularly if they are living a very different (often impoverished) existence in comparison to us. By practising this mode of ethical attention, Nussbaum argues that this assists in moral deliberation and decision making in our everyday lives. We can practise this mode of attention not only by listening compassionately to others with perspectives different from our own, but also by watching films or reading literature in which such scenarios are depicted in a sensitive and realistic manner.

By practising a loving attitude towards characters in works of fiction, we care about their plight. If we practise this moral attitude first in the safe fictional space, we can then apply it to real-life others we encounter. Yet, while it may be that we can cultivate positive moral habits through our engagement with *good* literature, surely the opposite may also be true, that some narrative artworks may undermine our understanding and morality. A causal account such as Nussbaum's may explain some of the fear associated with people, particularly vulnerable, young people, engaging with unethical or excessively violent fictional works or video games, and thereby also engaging with harmful messages depicted therein. Practising the virtues can cultivate effective habits which, in turn, become character traits and dispositions; yet, if this is true, then surely the same is true of vices.

As artworks are not inherently or essentially moral (or immoral), those engaging with such works should be critically engaged with whatever messages they are receiving. Being compassionate towards the characters and scenarios depicted in stories in insufficient; a reader must also adopt a critical appreciation of the work in question. This is particularly the case given that some works, and characters and situations depicted therein, require further critical analysis and ethical consideration. This is why I defend the attitude of critical perspectivism whereby moral agents are compassionate as well as critical of the various perspectives they encounter, whether these be fictional or otherwise. Note that to be critical thus is not the same as being cynical, which would seemingly be in tension with being compassionate.

Novels, films, or paintings may be sympathetic to their subject matter and encourage a loving attitude or ethical contemplation of an idea. They could also do the opposite. Artists may or may not be virtuous people. Those receiving the works may or may not be sensitively attuned to the relevant ethical nuances of the piece and they may or may not be educated as to how best comprehend or interpret the artwork in question. Furthermore, people may be inclined to link the aesthetic experiences they have in the theatre, cinema, bookstore or art gallery to their everyday experiences. All of this brings me to the point that it is not solely the artwork that we should focus on, even though considering these artworks and the experiences they afford is important. We also need to consider the person viewing, receiving, or engaging with the piece. If the work with which one is engaging may have a positive *or* negative message or effect, then we want individuals to be able to discern this and critically judge it. Adopting the ethical attitude of critical perspectivism entails the ability to critically analyse what one is viewing, and decide, in a reasonable and compassionate manner, how one ought to think about, and perhaps act upon or respond to (or not) not only the work itself but also the ideas and scenarios it represents.

The attitude of critical perspectivism becomes even more relevant when we consider artworks that are not paradigm examples of aesthetically and ethically good works. If a work is not designed to attune those who engage with them to ethically relevant nuances, or if it does not treat its subject matter in a caring manner, there may be all the more reason to be more critically than compassionately engaged with the work. This will also be true of mass artworks and messages received via other technological media such as social media and advertisements. Critical perspectivism is an attitude a moral agent adopts that requires the person receiving the art object or mass artwork or message conveyed via social media to be both critically and compassionately engaged with what they see and hear. This points to the need to strike a balance between being sceptical and considerate; between seeking truth and trying to understand what is intended by the person/s creating the work, or posting a comment, or 'sharing' an image, story, video or rumour. Ideally, the person receiving the communicated idea will be able to reasonably decide how best to interpret it along with how to respond to it – which may include acting upon what they have seen or heard. Yet the ease of determining an appropriate response may vary according to which medium is used to convey the message, how complex the message is and whether or not the creator of the message was being deceptive. In this way critical perspectivism may be seen as demanding yet may be practised and adopted as a good habit. For this reason, I focus on the response of those engaging with the work or message because this critical and compassionate response is the attitude I am at pains to describe and consider possible ways by which such an attitude may be educated. Critical perspectivism is the attitude we should adopt when engaging fairly and objectively with artworks, while also caring about the subject matter of the work, and the artist who created it. Critical perspectivism is also usefully directed towards mass art and media. Ideally, I would like to think that artists, journalists, technicians and general users of social media should adopt this attitude when they are creating works, writing articles, or posting comments online. Ultimately, critical perspectivism is an effective mode of interpreting information that comes 'at' us from many diverse sources.

Conclusion

Thus we can see how Nussbaum's 'loving attitude', her version of ethical attention, encourages a certain perspective to be adopted with reference to ethical situations and decision making. This loving attitude requires the moral agent to use their sympathetic imagination as well as their intellect in order to understand the facts of a particular situation and 'see' how to appropriately respond (Nussbaum, 2001, p. 66). In this chapter, we have seen Nussbaum (1990) defend two central claims. Firstly, that the view of life, and on how to live, conveyed by a text depends in part on the formal features of that text. From this it follows that the formal features of various sorts of literary texts may allow them to express different views on life and ways to live that cannot be expressed in other ways. The second claim is that there are some moral views which can be adequately expressed only through novels or narrative artworks, and therefore the study of such novels belongs within moral philosophy. The novels she considers to be good examples of moral philosophy are social realist works such as those of Charles Dickens and Henry James. One upshot of such a claim is to then defend the role of the humanities and the liberal arts tradition in a democratic society if we wish to have well rounded, flourishing citizens. Such democratic and reasonable citizens ideally have enhanced moral imaginations by being exposed to and engaging with various ethical scenarios and characters. Such an argument is at home amongst the supporters of democratic education and, within this liberal cosmopolitan view, it makes perfect sense. Yet in today's global society there must also be a consideration of the main sources of various narratives with which our citizens currently engage: namely, technologically mediated narratives that are shortened, sensationalised and/or transmitted via images. For these reasons, along with others that include individual differences in cognitive, emotional and experiential skill or ability, educators must seek to hone more than Nussbaum's ethical attitude of cognitive compassion in students. Critical perspectivism is required to ensure critical distance accompanies a compassionate concern for others and their stories no matter through which medium such stories are encountered.

While we may learn of the virtues through narrative artworks, we may ask whether other forms of media may also convey moral truths to those receiving and engaging with these stories, images and videos. We must also consider whether the opposite may also be true, that some works of literature, mass art, media and online information can undermine our ethical response to people, ideas and situations. As I have illustrated, practising the virtues makes effective habits which, in turn, become character; yet the same is true of vices. This would account for some of the fear associated with watching unethical mass artworks and engaging with harmful messages depicted therein. Virtue ethics is a good theory to utilise in order to explain and understand that practising virtuous behaviour is a positive thing. Upon this Aristotelian theory such behaviour enables us to lead a happy (flourishing) life and will see virtuous agents behaving kindly and compassionately to others. The flip side of such a theory sees vices practised also becoming ingrained and the nature or character of a person may be similarly affected in a retrograde manner.

There are many arguments that the media portrays morals that can be detrimental or have ill effects on viewers, particularly sensitive viewers such as children. We are all aware of the debates about violence, body image and intercultural relations. However, if a story and its images can teach us negative ideas, it may also be used as a tool for positive impact and the portrayal of morally sound ideas. Works of literature have long been deemed important to our culture – in part due to their moral content. The moral content of these narrative artworks teaches us about our common humanity by detailing situations and characters in writing and, in the case of film, through images, thereby allowing the specificity of moral scenarios to be conveyed. It is in observing these scenarios as well as interacting imaginatively with them, that we may learn from works of fiction. Yet even Nussbaum noted that the reader must already have a moral disposition if they are to feel appropriately caring responses towards characters. Moral formation occurs very early on and, in large part, in the home. So what role can educational institutions play in helping shape the moral attitude of children? One answer has been hinted at throughout this chapter – by offering certain texts that may be read and analysed, and by creating space for the imaginative engagement with stories. Yet we also need to be able to critically assess the stories we receive as well as the stories of which we are a part. I shall explore this further in chapter five, where I outline and defend the philosophy for children (P4C) pedagogy, including the community of inquiry (CoI), as one way in which to teach, model and habituate critical perspectivism.

As I have argued, we don't just want moral agents to learn how to be compassionate towards one another; we also require them to be critical thinkers who are creatively engaged with others, the environment and the world around them – online as well as face-to-face. Never has this been more important than in today's technologically mediated world whereby we have instant access to so many diverse points of view, images and sources of entertainment. In the next chapter, I explore how critical perspectivism applies to mass-produced and distributed narrative artworks such as film, mass art and other media. Critical perspectivism is an attitude that can be adopted when engaging with these other media platforms and mass art objects in an effort to support moral engagement with technologically mediated sources of information that are ubiquitous in the twenty-first century. On my account, critical perspectivism allows for and in fact requires and presumes shared human values or a sense of 'common humanity'. This compassionate respect for others can be easily forgotten when engaging with Web 2.0, particularly when users may need to adopt a critical stance towards avatars, bots, trolls, and the like. We do need to be critically engaged with technology, yet this does not eradicate the possibility of technology and mass art also offering us vehicles for moral engagement by providing us with the opportunity to compassionately engage with stories that differ from our own. Either way, critical perspectivism will be a useful moral attitude to adopt.

References

Aristotle. (1876). *The Nicomachean ethics*. London: Longmans, Green.

Blum, L. (1987). Compassion. In R. B. Kruschwitz and R. C. Roberts (Eds.), The virtues: Essays on moral character (pp. 229–236). Belmont: Wandsworth.

Carroll, N. (2000). Art and ethical criticism: An overview of recent directions of research. *Ethics, 110*(2), 350–387.

D'Olimpio, L., & Peterson, A. (2017). The ethics of narrative art: Philosophy in schools, compassion and learning from stories. *Journal of Philosophy in Schools, 4*(2). Special issue 'Why should Philosophy be taught in schools?' Ed. M. Hand.

Hepburn, R. W. (1990). Art, truth and the education of subjectivity. *Journal of Philosophy of Education, 24*, 185–198.

James, H. (1905). *The golden bowl*. London: Methuen & Company.

Kristjansson, K. (2007). *Aristotle, emotions, and education*. London: Routledge.

Magee, B. (1978). Philosophy and literature: Dialogue with Iris Murdoch. In B. Magee (Ed.), *Men of ideas*. London: British Broadcasting Corporation.

Murdoch, I. (1970). *The sovereignty of good*. London: Routledge & Kegan Paul. Chapter two, 'On "God" and "good".' In M. Warnock (Ed.), (1996). *Women philosophers*. London: Everyman & J. M. Dent.

Murdoch, I. (1998). *Existentialists and mystics: Writings on philosophy and literature* (P. J. Conradi, Ed.). New York: Allen Lane/The Penguin Press.

Nussbaum, M. C. (1990). *Love's knowledge: Essays on philosophy and literature*. Oxford: Oxford University Press.

Nussbaum, M. C. (1995). *Poetic justice: The literary imagination and public life.* Boston: Beacon Press.

Nussbaum, M. C. (1998). Exactly and responsibly: A defence of ethical criticism. *Philosophy and Literature, 22,* 343–365.

Nussbaum, M. C. (2001). *Upheavals of thought: The intelligence of emotions.* Cambridge: Cambridge University Press.

Nussbaum, M. C. (2010). *Not for profit: Why democracy needs the humanities.* Princeton, NJ: Princeton University Press.

Nussbaum, M. C. (2012). *The new religious intolerance: Overcoming the politics of fear in an anxious age.* Cambridge: The Belknap Press of Harvard University Press.

Peterson, A. (2016). *Compassion and education: Cultivating compassionate children, schools and communities.* London: Palgrave Macmillan.

Posner, R. A. (1997). Against ethical criticism. *Philosophy and Literature, 21*(1), 1–27.

Twain, M. (1884). *Adventures of Huckleberry Finn.* London: Chatto & Windus/orig. Charles L. Webster and Company.

Wilde, O. (1891). *The picture of Dorian Gray.* New York: W.W. Norton & Company, Inc.

Young, J. O. (2005). *Aesthetics: Critical concepts in philosophy.* London: Routledge.

3   Critical engagement

Having granted that compassion is an important part of a moral attitude one should adopt when seeking to make ethical decisions, it has also been acknowledged that moral agents must be critical of what they see and hear. Critical perspectivism is a moral attitude that requires both. The idea that we can learn from aesthetically and ethically good narrative artworks such as fine literature has been explored and supported, yet this claim is narrow and only defends the inclusion of certain artworks as central to the curriculum or moral philosophy. I am interested in exploring whether mass artworks may also be morally educative, given that these are works with which the majority of people, including children, engage. There are good reasons to think that technologically mediated information is to be approached with critical distance. Yet there is also good reason to note that engaging with others online should be done with compassion. The balance required or the weighting given to each is to be determined contextually, by the moral agent, in a particular time and place. Critical perspectivism allows for such situational discernment. In this way, the moral agent uses their rational mind and their imagination alongside rational emotions such as compassion when ascertaining the ethically relevant features of a scenario. This chapter further explores why a moral agent must be critical and cautious when negotiating technologically mediated sources of information, starting by considering the approaches taken towards mass art within the field of philosophical aesthetics.

Historically, the engagement of philosophy, particularly analytic philosophy, with mass art and media such as film and social media, has been, shall we say, reserved. Until very recently, philosophers in the Western tradition have been reluctant or conservative when it comes to embracing the serious philosophical consideration of entertainment mediums. When any such philosophising has been done it has typically been to serve as a warning of the depraved effects such media is likely to have on society and its members. The continental tradition has fared better, more readily engaging positively with such media, yet still focussing their attention on high art or avant-garde art rather than mass art or social media. Having said that, referring to the analytic/continental divide in philosophy is imperfect, as speaking in such clear-cut binary opposites is incomplete and doesn't allow for the philosophers that sit somewhere in the middle. Many contemporary philosophers speak of the need to blur the distinction between 'analytic' and 'continental' traditions, but there is still a pragmatic reality in applying such categories. I shall resist such strict categorisation myself, but this distinction is worth noting from the outset when considering the way philosophers have viewed technological advancements in media and how that is starting to alter. The truth is that philosophers should be engaged in reflecting on topics that have a significant impact upon people's everyday lives, and the meaning people make from engaging with mass art and media is certainly one predominant aspect of contemporary society.

It is worth commencing with this historical reflection because when it comes to talking philosophically about social media, online information and gaming, including augmented reality and multi-player games, philosophers are only just starting to write on such topics, and this mimics their reluctance previously to talk seriously about mass artworks such as film. Any reluctance is aided by the fact that technology is advancing at such a rapid rate, requiring academic scholarship to move quickly in order to keep up, and this is a cause for delay. Scholarship does not move particularly quickly, especially in philosophy. Yet perennial questions of personal identity, education and ethics are applicable and relevant to such contemporary topics, although I will be homing in on only a small part of what is available for consideration. Some of the aesthetic and ethical and associated educational concerns in relation to media are very similar to those that pertain to mass art. In fact, arguably, there are great overlaps between mass art and online entertainment and media. Therefore, an obvious starting point when discussing how people do and should engage with such media begins with considering what has been theorised about mass art and film.

As mass-produced and distributed entertainment forms started to become accessible and infiltrate the everyday for most people in the developed world, there was a noted resistance by philosophers of the twentieth century to take mass art seriously, either aesthetically or morally. Yet the need for mass art to be examined for both its moral and aesthetic possibilities is due, at least in part, to the predominance of mass art in society. Writing twenty years ago, Noel Carroll noted that when philosophers did consider mass art as part of their theories, they were "frequently dismissive and openly hostile" (Carroll, 1998, p. 15). Carroll argues that mass art should be taken seriously as art in its own right (*qua* art) because of its implications as well as its possibilities for society. Mass art, he claims, is here to stay and therefore deserves an adequate philosophical theory by which to categorise it and its place within general aesthetic theory (Carroll, 1998, p. 4). I concur and thus follow Carroll in classifying mass art as art, allowing certain works of mass art to be aesthetically 'good' when considered as works of art. Here is Carroll's definition of mass art:

X is a mass artwork if and only if:
(1) X is a multiple instance or type artwork
(2) which is produced and distributed by a mass technology
(3) and which artwork is intentionally designed to gravitate in its structural choices (for example its narrative forms, symbolism, intended affect and

even its content) toward those choices that promise accessibility with minimum effort, virtually on first contact, for the largest number of untutored (or relatively untutored) audiences.

(Carroll, 1998, p. 196)

It is easier today to defend Carroll's contention that mass art is a sub-category or extension of art proper and thus mass artworks are art *qua* art, even if it turns out that many instances of mass art are of a lower aesthetic and ethical quality than, for example, high- or avant-garde artworks. This recognition of the place mass art has within society, and therefore the need for aesthetic theory to include mass art within the category of art proper, is in part due to its ubiquitous nature and the fact that films and other mass artworks are indeed 'here to stay'. As such, philosophers are starting to engage with these mass artworks and theorise about them and their place within aesthetic theory. As Wartenberg notes:

I am struck by a sense of arrival . . . for the field of film and philosophy. When I began to argue that films could be relevant to philosophical concerns, that claim was met with a rather stony silence in the world of Anglo-American professional philosophy.

(Wartenberg, 2007, preface)

In fact, much of the current philosophy of film literature pursues an optimistic approach that may be identified with Walter Benjamin's hope for the art of the masses. This optimism sees film as a vehicle for screening philosophical thought experiments and offering new perspectives on issues that have relevance to everyday life by engendering critical consciousness. If films allow for philosophical thinking, then they encourage social, political and economic critique of social norms. Yet most popular films that are digested in large quantities are Hollywood or Bollywood blockbuster films that are generally criticised for depicting stereotypes and for eliciting formulaic emotions (Collingwood, 1969, p. 57). Theorists who conceive of cinema as a means of thinking must firstly reply to the objections that most films are formulaic and do not encourage active, intelligent, or imaginative participation.

One prominent philosopher who not only rejected the idea that mass artworks could encourage critical thinking but, further, worried that such texts would promote passive spectatorship and, by extension, passive citizenship, was T. W. Adorno. Having witnessed the damaging, brain-washing effect of Nazi propaganda, Adorno's concern was that mass-produced and distributed artworks, including Hollywood Studio films, portrayed social norms as uncontestable and stereotypes as natural and therefore immutable. He argued that the filmic medium portrayed a particular homogeneous image of life that was presented in a 'flattened' manner to the viewer who consumed it whole, without pausing to consider whether or not it was true or good. In contrast to other artworks, Adorno claimed that mass art did not allow for critical or imaginative engagement with ideas depicted therein, and such narratives could further reinforce existing stereotypes and dubious social mores. It must be noted that the films being produced by Hollywood at the time Adorno was writing were indeed formulaic and commissioned, censored and controlled by a relatively small group of powerful, conservative, white men. Times have certainly changed, and mass artworks now represent a wider variety of perspectives, even while the film and television industry is still largely dominated by men. However, even while there are many different stories being told in contemporary culture, via television, film and social media, the focus on the critical thinker, the interpreter of the narrative, is vital. If mass art and media can engage viewers critically, this is positive, yet, if most viewers are uncritically ingesting such media, and the messages and stereotypes therein contained, the question remains as to whether Adorno is correct and whether this is cause for concern.

Adorno may have overstated the worry he had for uncritical reflection on mass art, yet his desire to encourage critical reflection is valid, and a sentiment that is shared by Benjamin. As Miriam Hansen notes:

> Abandoning his defensive stance against the cinema as a mass media, Adorno can even conceive of a "liberated" film which would have to "extricate its *a priori* collectivity from the mechanisms of unconscious and irrational influence" and enlist it "in the service of emancipatory intentions". Benjamin would not have disagreed.
>
> (1981, p. 192)

It is worth reading Adorno alongside Benjamin in order to defend a moderate approach to mass art and media that focusses on critical engagement with such narratives.

Film, as a technological art form, can be viewed and understood by many people virtually on first contact (Carroll, 2004, pp. 486–487) and can elicit powerful responses. This is also true of many images shared via social media and reality television, which is enormously popular even when it lacks any substantive plot. The nature of the audience's various responses to mass art and media is still under debate, but includes responding to the emotional quality of film, images and realistic representations (Wartenberg, 2007, p. 5) that can depict various aspects of society, character and politics. Following the influence of Deleuze, much of the current philosophy of film literature is optimistic with regards to the potential of films to explore philosophical ideas. The cinematic experience is powerful because it combines sensory input with story to convey social, political and emotional truths. As Colman states:

> The audio-visual nature of certain cinema . . . achieves 'a victory' over th[e] heirarchization of modes and concepts of art. This is also a victory in philosophical terms for art as a political form that contributes something to the world.
>
> (2011, p. 253)

This idea that film can provide a social commentary and thus be meaningful, as opposed to mindless, is an aspect of the contemporary Deleuzean approach to film that reflects the optimism that emerges from Benjamin, who celebrates the potential of films to screen ideas. Yet the stronger claim that can be read from Benjamin's writings, that critical detachment is somehow built into mass media because audiences watching films are distracted (Benjamin, 1969, p. 240), should be reconsidered. Adorno and Horkheimer's warnings of possible ill effects of cinema, such as the passivity of its viewers and the economic motivation of blockbuster films, need to be re-examined and juxtaposed with Benjamin's view. Neither Benjamin or Adorno and Horkheimer are completely correct, yet both positions are valuable to consider in relation to the ethical aspects of film spectatorship. Furthermore, these same considerations apply to mass media and social media.

Osborne and Charles remark that "the ecstatic character of Benjamin's political thought at the outset of the 1930s, sees technology appear on a political knife-edge between its possibilities as "a fetish of doom" and "a key to happiness" (2011). Film, when fetishised, is focussed on making money or promoting an ideology rather than telling stories as a narrative art form. Carroll notes, "Perhaps the greatest anxieties about mass art concern morality" (1998, p. 291). Similar concerns apply to other technologically mediated sources of information, games and products. For instance, the debate as to whether or not augmented reality games are beneficial or a cause for concern emerged in 2016 with the release of PokémonGO to widespread up-take, as augmented reality games became playable by anyone with a smartphone. The moral concern is that augmented reality games turn real and even sacred spaces into virtual gaming arenas, and the distracted player of such games forgets not only the importance of the physical reality of where they are playing (players have endangered themselves by falling off cliffs while playing PokémonGO!) but also face-to-face connections with friends, family and strangers. The counter-argument is that such a cultural phenomenon provides a commonality to increase a sense of community amongst people using these public spaces in this way, and gets them out and about and moving while gaming, rather than traditional methods whereby players sit for hours in front of a computer screen indoors (ABC Radio National, The Minefield, 2016; Chalmers, 2016).

These entertainment forms, and the creation and sale of games, films and television series and advertisements, smartphone apps and the like, must be recognised to be motivated by economic reasons as well as ideological ones. By re-reading Adorno alongside Benjamin, we are reminded of the ability mass art and media have to manipulate and be used as an economic and political apparatus, as well as a vehicle for harmless entertainment and, possibly, insight and even wisdom. Even though Adorno does not envision the potential and possibility of film in the way that Benjamin speculated and Deleuze celebrated, his concerns should not be dismissed as ignorant or unwarranted. Film, as an art of the masses, embedded within society and used by social, political, moral humans, has the potential to be constructive *or* destructive. So too do other mass art and media.

It must be noted that, using Carroll's definition, mass artworks include magazines, blockbuster movies, novels, television programs and (some) advertisements. Carroll distinguishes instances of mass art from examples of mass culture such as cooking shows, news coverage and sports events, which, he claims, are not artworks. This definition of mass art seems accurate, although broad, yet the distinction between mass art and mass culture appears arbitrary and is almost made redundant when Carroll notes that identifying a mass artwork as opposed to an object of mass culture is simply a matter of asking, "what else could it be?" (Carroll, 1998, p. 197). One example of how we could categorise something as an instance of mass culture as opposed to mass art is the Japanese super chef show, *Iron Chef*. *Iron Chef* is a popular, competitive cooking show and, despite its entertainment value, and the fact that it's televised in many countries, it is an example of mass culture, not of mass art on Carroll's definition.

This seems to be a case of correct categorisation in the instance of *Iron Chef*. However, some cases may be more difficult to categorise, for instance a beautifully shot advert produced by a movie director, such as the television advertisement for Chanel No. 5 perfume featuring a famous actress. Some may want to argue that this is an example of mass art as it plays like a mini-Hollywood feature film (and had a similar budget). Carroll's definition allows an argument to be made that this advert is indeed a mass artwork, yet it would not be as simple as asking, 'what else could it be?' Such a question would not always readily solve the dilemma of categorising borderline cases that straddle the mass culture/mass art divide. The standard of an ideal audience member may be relied upon here in order to provide an authoritative guide when dealing with borderline cases. This ideal critic would be someone who is familiar with the artworld and its historicity (as Levinson, 2004, p. 35 refers to it) as well as the intentional element of the work in question in order to ascertain the mass-produced and distributed product's place within the realm of art. They should be able to judge whether or not a product is an instance of mass art or mass culture.

Having said that, as our technology allows for multimedia and social media platforms to be increasingly integrated into our form of communicating and receiving information, the blurring distinctions between advertisements, product placement, product endorsement and popularity means that we are less able to discern when we are being 'sold' something and, worse, we are almost always being sold something. As advertisers increasingly try to sell us ideas about what we could *be* and how our lives could *be* rather than things we *use*, the subtle impact of advertising is less evident to us even as it is increasingly effective and persuasive. As analytics are collected to provide precious information about user demographics and preferences to advertisers and companies, search engines such as Google are wielding huge amounts of data that can attract a high sum. This raises concerns about privacy and also about the kind of information that is valuable, the kind which can be bought and sold in the name of the free market and neoliberal agenda. In this neoliberal marketplace, everything becomes reduced to its functional and use value, values that have an attached quantifiable price tag. In this political economy, we forget to value things such as knowledge *for its own sake*, and education, the arts and the humanities suffer as a result. Such slippage highlights the increasing need for consumers to be critically engaged with the forms of mass art and culture they are, quite literally, buying into.

Mass art moves further away from the aesthete's formalist definition of art *qua* Art that was detailed in the last chapter. Carroll (1988; 1993; 1994) defends a historical characterisation of art and then offers a functional account of mass art. He defends the compatibility of these two approaches and argues against inconsistency in his theory, stating that, as mass art is a different category to art in general, certain forms of art can be understood functionally as well as historically. Certainly the functional component of mass art is often what is under attack or the subject of debate when we examine the mass-produced and distributed nature of mass artworks. These works are designed to affect large numbers of people, with detractors arguing that the function of mass art is simply to profit, rather than primarily to serve any aesthetic purpose. As a sub-category of Art proper, mass art differs from 'popular art' or art that is popular, even though mass art often is popular. Carroll argues that mass art is not the same as 'popular art', even if some mass artworks are immensely popular and consumed in large numbers by mass audiences. The reason the term 'popular art' is misleading when referring to mass art is that it does not encompass the historicity of mass art in relation to art generally, making it difficult to delineate the boundaries of the category of mass art. Carroll explains, "the type of production that concerns us has a certain historical specificity. 'Popular art' is an ahistorical term" (Carroll, 1998, p. 185). He further notes that

> [Mass art] has arisen in the context of modern industrial mass society and it is expressly designed for use by that society, employing, as it does, the characteristic productive forces of that society – namely, mass technologies of production and distribution – in order to deliver art to enormous consuming populations – populations that are 'mass' in the sense that they cross national, class, religious, political, ethnic, racial and gender boundaries.
>
> (Carroll, 1998, p. 185)

Given the blurring between mass art and mass cultural and media objects, this functional account applies to mass media and social media as well as mass art. Applying a 'family resemblances' approach to art, as Weitz does in a Wittgensteinian fashion (2004, p. 15), allows for new sub-categories of art to be formed as the need arises. As new conditions and cases arise (such as mass art, for instance) which demand a decision by those theoretically inclined as to whether or not they fit into the concept of art or whether or not the concept should be extended to include such instances, the concept may be tested in order to see if it allows for the inclusion of this new, possible subset of art proper. For example, a case may be made for including selfies as a mass art sub-category of self-portraiture. Selfies, the act of taking one's own picture and usually sharing it via social media platforms, may be considered as art, even when it may be claimed that many selfies are not very good, aesthetically, when compared to traditional self-portraits.

The creative, innovative and expansive nature of art and technology sees new (physical and virtual) objects constantly being created. When we apply Carroll's definition of mass art, incorporate Weitz's Wittgensteinian reliance on family resemblances and include Levinson's 'essential historicity', this allows for the blurring between categories and the fact that sometimes particular instances will be instances of both mass art and social media. Selfies may well be an example of this. The creative nature of art allows for this movement, as media elements are incorporated into Art proper and vice versa. The photographs on Instagram may well be deemed art, yet this does not necessarily mean that all social media examples are instances of art (mass or otherwise). Therefore, each instance may involve asking, as Carroll does, 'what else would it be', but the answer may not be obvious and may require defending (much as Duchamp's urinal and Warhol's soup cans have required defending in the past, even when displayed in an art gallery). The object in question may well belong to more than one category, and it is for this I allow.

What is of interest, in the context of this book, and regardless of their classification, is how mass art, media and technology may be used and their impact in society. Their power and impact are interesting precisely because of the widespread engagement with such media objects. Benjamin acknowledges the potential for mass art to manipulate, yet he contends that mass art is progressive in its ability to transform human perception, not by expressing or emblematising it, but by encouraging its evolution (Carroll, 1998, p. 122). For Benjamin, film allows the viewer to stand outside of it, critically. This is due to the camera work as mediator between actor and viewer that "permits the audience to take the position of a critic, without experiencing any personal contact with the actor" (Benjamin, 1969, pp. 228–229). As an aside, the influence of Bertolt Brecht and Sergei Eisenstein in this approach is critiqued by Adorno, who is wary of Benjamin's use of these theorists in supporting a strong claim about the emancipatory power of film (Osborne, 2008, p. 63).

From Benjamin we learn that the power of film may be harnessed once we have recognised the mechanisms of the apparatus (Benjamin, 1991–1999, pp. 107–108), but he does not reduce film solely to a means of either empowering *or* attempting to monopolise viewers with images depicted *en masse*. Osborne and Charles (2011) note that Benjamin's writings on film are justly renowned for their twin theses of the transformation of the concept of art by its 'technical reproducibility' and the new possibilities for collective experience this contains, in the wake of the historical decline of the 'aura' of the work of art, a process that film is presented as definitively concluding. While this more traditional art aura regresses, there is also the chance, Benjamin suggests, of a newly liberated 'distracted' viewer who is progressive, keeping up with the new, active filmic techniques (Markus, 2001, p. 17). Certainly with the advent of social media and smart technology, we as modern-day viewers are more distracted than ever previously. Yet Adorno's concern that new media will lead to a dystopia should give us pause to think more deeply about the impact of this new technology, of mass art and social media in particular, on viewers.

Adorno is keen to point out that artworks should challenge the viewer to pause and critically receive an idea or engage with a new perspective. This critical distance is an important aspect of the aesthetic experience. Yet, with mass art and media, it appears as though much of the time we are simply invited to hedonistically indulge in pleasure. There is nothing inherently wrong with this use of leisure time, but the question we can still investigate asks what messages are being promoted and reinforced by the texts or media with which we engage. For Adorno, who is concerned with the aesthetic value of unique artworks, the loss of aura is not cause to celebrate; the technologically reproducible artwork is not as valuable because it does not challenge the viewer to actively engage with the picture of society it presents. In this way, mass artworks are unlike so-called 'high' or avant-garde artworks, and thus lack ethical as well as aesthetic value. Adorno and Horkheimer state, "The double mistrust of traditional culture as ideology is combined with the mistrust of industrialized culture as a swindle" (p. 161).

Adorno has been criticised as being elitist, and his writings on jazz certainly do nothing to defend him from this claim (McCann, 2008, pp. 12–13). However, it must be noted that the sense of value to which he refers is not simply aesthetic, but also social and political. With the benefit of hindsight, if we acknowledge that Adorno was overly critical of the culture industry and over-stated his ethical and social concerns with regards to the passivity of viewers, some of his critique is still salvageable and relevant to the contemporary debate. Furthermore, it is important to read Adorno's theory in its context of Hitler taking control of Germany in the 1930s and the Nazi effort to eliminate art that challenged the political picture of the Weimar Republic they wished to sustain. Having witnessed the effect of propaganda in Nazi Germany and moving to America to form the Frankfurt School, Adorno and Horkheimer bore witness to the rise of the Hollywood Studio Film system in Post-WWII America. Writing in the 1930–1950s, they worried about the ethical impact of the culture industry on society and the lack of diverse narratives being screened. While the current social and political climate is much changed, their focus on the moral impact of engaging with mass-produced and distributed products of a media industry is still of relevance today. The alleged lack of value (aesthetic and ethical) and the promotion of negative values (e.g. hyper-nationalism) of mass-consumed artworks require examination, even if not all such mass artworks are guilty of Adorno's criticisms. Furthermore, there is still the criticism of Hollywood today as lacking in diversity in its depictions and roles for women, minorities, and older actors (particularly actresses).

The writings of both Benjamin and Adorno are relevant in our technological society with its blurry lines between art, media and technological sharing platforms. We can value the different stories being told in contemporary culture, but we must also be mindful of the context in which these stories are conveyed and received. The viewer's meaning-making may be constructive or destructive, as the creative force has the potential for both. An obvious example of this is the fine line that separates propaganda from entertainment, whereby we cannot always tell the difference in product or affect (Riefenstahl, 1935; Devereaux, 1998). With everyone as a potential contributor to online dialogue, we each have the ability to encourage a positive (life-affirming) or a negative (life-denying) response to people, events and the earth itself, so it is important that we encourage and educate or train critical as well as appropriately compassionate spectatorship of mass art, media and social media.

Where is the place for the thinking viewer in the cinema?

This optimism of the power of film to think and encourage thinking is taken up by contemporary philosophers such as Thomas Wartenberg, who see film as a vehicle for screening philosophical thought experiments and offering new perspectives on issues that (may) have relevance to everyday life. Wartenberg claims that "film is able to give philosophical concepts and ideas a human garb that allows their consequences to be perceived more clearly" (2007, p. 5) and "films can *make arguments, provide counterexamples* to philosophical claims, and *put forward novel philosophical theories*" (2007, p. 9). If films allow for philosophical thinking, then they are like some other so-called 'high' artworks in that they encourage social, political and economic critique of social norms. If contemporary films depict diverse narratives instead of constructing a homogeneous picture of social reality, then audiences are encouraged to think critically by imaginatively engaging with multiple perspectives, thereby alleviating Adorno's fear of passivity. Yet Adorno's (albeit overstated) concerns are still worthy of discussion. Many, if not most, popular films that are digested in large quantities promote stereotypes with dubious moral values. Wartenberg is correct to claim that some films are philosophical, yet he gives examples of Hollywood blockbusters to support his claim, though it is mostly these films that are subject to the Adornian criticism. Hollywood blockbuster films that are screened ubiquitously and make the most revenue are the kinds of mass-produced and distributed works to which Adorno objects. Theorists who conceive of cinema as a means of thinking must still reply to the objection that most films simply do not encourage active, intelligent, imaginative participation with the stereotypes therein depicted. While this does not demolish claims that films can somehow 'do' philosophy, the acknowledgement that film may encourage critical reception must not discount the caution offered by Adorno.

Wartenberg acknowledges how realistic and convincing the depictions are through the filmic medium, yet he doesn't acknowledge the criticism of this very same quality. For Wartenberg, the life-like quality of films allows the viewer to be absorbed in the narrative. Yet it is this same feature that results in many blockbuster films resisting imaginative engagement by presenting their story in a manner so all-inclusive that there is less room to imagine it differently. Most blockbuster films depict stories in approximately 90–120 minutes, tying up loose ends in order to leave a feeling of resolution with the viewer. The viewer is not given the time to reflect on the story while watching it, as they may do when reading a book, which adds to the sense that the story is immutable. A screened story is often designed to be ingested as a whole, invoking base emotional responses such as revenge, sadness, romance etcetera without encouraging any critique of the context (either that of the viewer or the scenario depicted within the film) that elicits these feelings (Levine, 2001, pp. 63–71). Film is almost always designed to be accessible. While this in itself is not a bad thing, accessibility often means that detailed argument is lost and 'watered down' due to the compressed nature of film. Admittedly, films do not have to be simplified in this manner, but many, particularly blockbusters, are, and these are the most watched films. Even Wartenberg acknowledges that structural avant-garde films:

> are made for a small, intellectual audience, not for the huge audience that Hollywood films aim to reach. As a result, they are more hermetic, harder to watch and understand, and call for a very different type of attention than do standard fiction films.
>
> (2007, p. 117)

From Wartenberg's comment it may be discerned that, in contrast to avant-garde films, blockbusters are designed to be easier to watch and understand, precisely because they are targeted at large audiences. It is accepted that there are auteurs who knowingly engage with philosophical ideas and portray them through film, yet even these films cannot 'do philosophy' without the audience actively participating in the experience and reflecting on the ideas presented. Such reflection may occur either while watching the film or afterwards, and it must be admitted that there are going to be audience members who simply *never* reflect upon the ideas presented or context that elicited their emotional response(s). The quote above also makes mention of the kind of attention called for, from the spectator, to appropriately receive the film. I would suggest that viewers watching films philosophically, and those watching philosophical films, are already critical thinkers, which explains their attraction to philosophical films which require of them this 'very different type of attention'.

A crucial aspect of film's raison d'être is to be seen, engaged with and received. If only some films allow for critique of social, political and economic norms and these films are attended by critical viewers, then how is film more generally a tool for thinking? Furthermore, critical thinkers may attend and enjoy films that do not encourage or elicit any such critical examination of what is conveyed. As such, these critical thinkers may not be *critically* engaged with, for instance, a formulaic romantic comedy. Instead, such a viewer may be watching the rom-com precisely for the 'base' or 'canned' emotional response such a film is designed to evoke. If a large proportion of cinema-going audiences are viewing formulaic Hollywood blockbusters for pure entertainment, then they may not be watching such movies in order to be challenged to think critically about philosophical ideas. Wartenberg acknowledges this criticism and replies as follows with reference to Charles Chaplin's *Modern Times* (1936):

> Still, the objector might persist, even if you are right about that, viewers do not watch the Chaplin film for its philosophical insights, but for its humor. Although you might be able to squeeze some philosophy out of its portrayal

of the assembly line, we are not interested in the film for that, but rather for Chaplin's amazing antics. Here, I can only agree that Chaplin's comic riffs are an important source of our interest in *Modern Times*. But I would go on to point out that the humor of the sequence I have been discussing is intimately bound up with the thought that the human being is functioning as a machine, mechanically. . . . As I see it, you cannot separate the film's serious thinking about alienation from its comic portrayal in order to deny that the film involves a philosophically significant contribution.

(2006, p. 30)

Wartenberg claims that, in order to understand the film and appreciate its humour, you are already thinking about the philosophical concepts of human and machine. Yet the viewer may not reflect on arguments about industrialisation in order to laugh at the film and, as such, they may not be 'doing philosophy'. In order to be 'doing philosophy', surely the viewer has to be aware that they are thinking about the philosophical concept under discussion. If there is no reflection on a concept, in this instance, on the concept of mechanisation and the human as automaton, then this is not an instance of philosophical thinking. Wartenberg is suggesting that, to understand the humour, you also have to understand the concept philosophically, i.e. the idea of the human as automaton. However, if philosophical thinking is broadened out as Wartenberg here describes, then family resemblance is lost and any kind of mental activity that involves thinking becomes 'doing philosophy'. Philosophy, in this way, ceases to be recognised as reflective thinking that involves considering arguments, counter-arguments and responses. As we have already seen, Wartenberg acknowledges that these elements are necessary for philosophy. While some films may be able to philosophise in this manner, if the spectator isn't aware of the arguments being made, can it be claimed that the spectator is doing philosophy simply by laughing at the images depicted? Similarly, we can imagine someone reading a peer-reviewed philosophy paper published in a journal article and not understanding a word of it. I would also claim that this person is not doing philosophy either.

The point being made here is that, regardless of the source of the information or images being received, the important focus remains on the person who is engaging with these sources. Whether or not the source material is good, aesthetically or ethically, is not as important as whether the viewer is receiving the message critically or passively. In pointing to the ethical concern about passive spectatorship, Adorno may sound pessimistic, but this worry must be taken as seriously as the celebration of mass art as a democratising force to bring positive messages to widespread audiences. As the work itself is neither inherently positive nor negative, we must ask how we can encourage critical engagement with mass art and media.

What we can learn from Adorno

Prior to the publication of Deleuze's cinema books, theorists like Adorno and Horkheimer feared the advent of the Hollywood Studio film as akin to Nazi propaganda. Dismissed as elitist, their concern was that mass-produced and distributed artworks portrayed depicted social mores as immutable reality. If the viewer's imagination cannot critically engage with film, i.e. through montage or similar 'shock' techniques, then viewers cannot critique the moral and social status quo screened; instead, they simply receive it, and it is reinforced. Concerned that technology within a capitalist framework allows for mass-produced and distributed artworks to be formulaically churned out, creating a culture industry, Adorno claims in 'Culture Industry Revisited':

> although the culture industry undeniably speculates on the conscious and unconscious states of the millions towards which it is directed, the masses are not primary, but secondary, they are an object of calculation; an appendage to the machinery. The customer is not king, as the culture industry would have us believe, not its subject but its object.
>
> (p. 13)

Adorno's hostility towards the culture industry is evident, but times have changed and, enabled by the digital revolution, mass art and television series in particular are being revitalised and coming into their own as they offer interesting and multi-faceted characters and narratives. Yet, amongst this relatively newfound enthusiasm for film by analytic philosophers, it must be acknowledged that much of mass-produced and distributed art is primarily aimed at commercial success as opposed to encouraging critical spectatorship. It is therefore still worth considering what messages – for instance, about sex, class and race – are being depicted and received. And if art is simply imitating life, we should further consider what the cost might be of continuing to present and passively accept existing social, class and racial discriminations.

The idea that values are embedded in film is not new or controversial. Defining values as generalised, cross-situational dispositions to act in certain ways, Barry Brummett claims that values can show through form in film, even without the medium being exclusively linguistic (2013, p. 62). Films convey values to the audience through the way they conclude a narrative, depict images and scenes, and enhance mood through lighting, sound and visual effects (Brummet, 2013, p. 66). Relying on the notions of homology as tied to ideology, Brummett explains that:

> This idea of homology can be a way to understand how texts may appeal to values without ever linguistically articulating them. Predispositions to respond to and to judge, socially held guides for choices, all the things that values "are", may be activated at a formal level. This is not the same thing as being brought to conscious awareness, because we are so often not fully aware of how form is working in our texts and our experiences. Like ideology, form is most powerful when it is most invisible, and that is most of the time.
>
> (p. 64)

Brummett suggests that we read films through their formal features in the same way we read and understand social contexts. Films are life-like, and viewers have a shared understanding of social expression which comprises non-verbal as well as linguistic conventions. As such, we communicate and gather meaning, including values, from film in much the same way as we do in everyday life. For example, the first scene in a romantic comedy where the protagonist meets or sees the character with whom they will eventually form a romantic relationship will be shot in a certain way with specific music and lighting and the body language of the characters will indicate to viewers that this is the relationship we are watching to see how it unfolds (which is, often, predictably). This ideal of a 'soul mate' may then play out in the film, suggesting that the ideal relationship is one that overcomes odds and ends 'happily ever after'.

Adorno was concerned about the homogenising effect of the culture industry, which depicted specific social and moral messages. Adorno did not allow space for critical engagement with mass artworks. In creating products for consumer consumption, Adorno claims that the mass-produced and distributed artworks are all different, yet all the same, creating a homogenised product that is willingly ingested by the masses. Adorno explains:

> Illusory universality is the universality of the art of the culture industry, it is the universality of the homogeneous same, an art which no longer even promises happiness but only provides easy amusement as relief from labour.
>
> (1997, p. 7)

Adorno's concern does not apply to every film, yet there are certainly formulaic and homogeneous stories told and re-told through mass artworks. If we consider Hollywood blockbuster romance films, and apply Brummett's technique of reading the patterned rhetorical messages throughout a few of them, we reach this same conclusion. Whereas Brummett claims the message is not explicitly argued for, he details readings of films that give rise to certain values embedded in the form of the films (p. 67). This is evident in romantic comedies that have a predictable plot line of girl meets boy, girl is not interested in boy, there is an event that causes them to have to work together in some manner, and they eventually fall for each other, only being reunited and professing their love at the last minute after encountering a number of obstacles designed to separate them. The values of 'true love conquers all' and the idea of taking a 'leap of faith', as love is truly love only if you have to risk something in order to pursue it are common themes in such films. The interesting question is what, if any, effect do such stories have on viewers?

Certainly, Adorno overstates his claim and his view is too extreme, as evidenced when he writes that even those viewers attempting to engage with mass art actively or critically are only ever enacting a pseudo-active voice and are doomed to ineffectual rebellion against such stories. Adorno writes, "whenever they attempt to break away from the passive status of compulsive consumers and 'activate' themselves, they succumb to pseudo-activity (Adorno & Horkheimer, 1997, pp. 52–53)." Adorno here is referring to acts of rebellion, such as 'writing letters of complaint' that are ineffectual against the mass culture industry. These days, however, there is much power to be had in the voice of the dissatisfied consumer who makes use of social media in order to express their perspective. The viewer can be critical and express an active voice. However, despite his lack of recognition of the power of the individual spectator, Adorno's belief that mass consumerism forms an economic urge to create easily digestible works for the lowest common denominator must not be disregarded. The 'rom-com' is a case in point. The viewer may be critical of the film's story, yet is likely to have the relevant emotions at the end when the couple finally overcome adversity and admit their love for each other. As the music swells, there is a close-up of two smiling faces, and even the cynical viewer is moved. They may not apply this belief in soul mates to their own life, but they may feel the burden of the stereotype each time they are asked why they 'aren't married yet' or when are they 'going to settle down?'

Adorno first claimed in *The Culture Industry* that the masses seek and love the rules by which they are bound by buying in to mass cultural commodities and their associated ideals. It is certainly the case that the culture industry has acquired and maintained immense social, political and economic power. Even when we knowingly engage with products of this culture industry such as Reality TV, gossip magazines, sartorialist street style blogs and relentless Twitter feeds, are we not still buying in to that machine? Adorno is wrong to claim that the viewer is almost always completely passive and cannot counter the narrative and its associated values screened. With the advent of social media, viewers are critiquing and satirising the mass cultural products even as they voraciously consume them. However, as Brummett details, the subtle messages of values and ideology are screened and do reinforce existing social values. Brummett explains:

> Values are rarely, if ever, explicitly articulated in the films, and if they are, it is in the context of arguments about how to deal with instant rabies rage virus – hardly the sort of relevance one encounters in everyday life. Yet I think the homology obtained across the films, the audience's experience of the medium, and the audience's experience of the strange urban context likely invokes a sense of values and their application.
>
> (p. 66)

Brummett's explanation of the homogenised messages and values that pervade films is tied to the understanding that films are created by social, moral and political people and companies. Likewise, there is an understanding of the seemingly obvious point that the reason viewers understand films is that they too understand the social context of which they are also a part. This more subtle reading of how film influences viewers is compatible with the ethical concern described by Adorno. Although Adorno's original thesis is too strong, his worry is still recognisable with reference to spectatorship today.

Adorno's point that ought to be remembered is that mass artworks are created in a political, social and economic context and they influence the society which sustains them. One aim of Hollywood films is to keep the attention of mass audiences in a bid to retain their economic contribution. One way this is achieved is by not challenging certain stereotypes that attract mainstream and widespread audiences. These stereotypes have embedded values linked to ideological contexts. While there is room within the dominant capitalist ideology for diversity, capitalism seeks to remain dominant and therefore does not allow *a great deal* of diversity. As Adorno observes, the value of creative autonomy is the expression of diverse perspectives. This idea is summed up by Thomas Osborne, who writes, "the idea of creative autonomy here is an ethical idea rather than a substantive notion: a regulative ideal rather than an accomplishable goal" (2008, p. 9). Adorno uses the word autonomy, Osborne claims, as a speculative notion as opposed to a concrete goal. This is to say that the word is not formally defined, yet advocates striving for autonomy and creative expression as opposed to uniformity. The more the culture industry allows for diverse narratives and values, the more creative it is. This allows for critical spectatorship.

Throughout his writings it is evident that Adorno's thought evolves as reflected in his conversations and letters to Walter Benjamin and Siegfried Kracauer (Adorno & Benjamin, 1999). In 'The Culture Industry Revisited', Adorno slightly modifies his initial claim that audiences are completely passive, asserting that audiences do mistrust authority, which allows them to distinguish between art (or mass art) and reality. Several years later when interviewed on the radio, Adorno seemed surprised that the masses were able to "critically assess the political and social implications of the event" (Hansen, 1981–1982, p. 60), in this case the wedding of Dutch Princess Beatrix to a German diplomat. He was forced to conclude that complete manipulation of the masses by those in power via the culture industry is not possible. Similarly, he acknowledged that the consciousness of the masses is (or could be) varied, multiple and dynamic.

This theoretical progress Adorno makes reflects the changes in mass art at the time he is writing, from the monopoly of the Hollywood Studio system in the 1930s and 1940s to the increased diversification in the industry. From my perspective, this progress also increases the plausibility of Adorno's ethical, political and economic concerns with regard to mass art. Although Adorno's conclusions are overstated and draw from a specific cultural context, his ethical concerns should not be so quickly dismissed. While it may not be the case that monopolising capitalist and consumerist forces will eventually ensure that we homogenise until we are devoid of individuality and distinction, the threat of being encouraged to passively ingest 'facts' from a variety of technological sources without critical reflection is a worrying prospect. This prospect is grounds for acknowledging Adorno's later essay 'Transparencies on Film' as encouraging a subtle re-think of cinema as produced and displayed in an ideological context.

In this later article, Adorno claims:

> In its attempt to manipulate the masses the ideology of the culture industry itself becomes as internally antagonistic as the very society which it aims to

control. The ideology of the culture industry contains the antidote to its own life. No other plea could be made for its defense.

(p. 202)

Films allow for diverse voices to be heard and screened, Adorno now acknowledges in 'Transparencies on Film'. In this way, the culture industry gives expression to repressed or minority values which could possibly rise up against the dominant ideology if not given an outlet. Yet, even if various voices are depicted, it is the dominant values that are ultimately reinforced. For example, "while intention is always directed against the playboy, the dolce vita and wild parties, the opportunity to behold them seems to be relished more than the hasty verdict" (pp. 201–202). In depicting these images, Adorno claims, the culture industry reinforces them. Adorno notes the complexity of the relationship between film and society. If technology and cinema go hand in hand, so too do accompanying social values. Adorno claims, "There could be no aesthetics of the cinema, not even a purely technological one, which would not include the sociology of the cinema" (p. 202). In this way, cinema cannot be purely aesthetic; it must also link to society and with social concerns.

Continuing the conversation with Walter Benjamin

When critiquing social, political and economic factors that influence the production and up-take of mass artworks, it is useful to read Adorno alongside Benjamin. Benjamin offers an optimistic account of the (politically, socially and personally) emancipatory potential of art as it develops technologically in a modern context, even though he also recognises that the modern world fetishises commodities by using them for their economic value and political and social power. Osborne details Benjamin's attitude to mass art:

Because modern experience just *is* technological it is right that art itself should be expressive of this. Art can serve as a means of mastering the elemental forces of a technological second nature. Photography and film accustom humanity to the new apperceptions conditioned by technology. Technological art – like film and photography – becomes the site of exploration of future relations between technology and the human.

(p. 60)

Certainly this has been proven as technology continues to advance and our use of it builds upon existing modes of self-expression. Benjamin and Adorno agreed that, in comparison to Art proper, the technological reproduction of mass art strips the artwork of its 'aura' or unique artistic quality. Adorno argues that the loss of the aura of a work of art results in the simultaneous erosion of the artwork's aesthetic value. Yet this is not the case for Benjamin. As Osborne articulates, for Benjamin, "contrary to Adorno, the end of the aura is not necessarily negative in its consequences" (p. 61). However, Benjamin is not offering a directly oppositional thesis to Adorno. Benjamin acknowledges that there are many social effects in response to mass art, one being that "the film responds to the shriveling of the aura with an artificial build-up of the "personality" outside the studio" (1969, p. 224). Benjamin could have been predicting the rise of the self-imaging with which many users of social media are fixated. Current technology allows ordinary people to similarly represent themselves as if they were stars. The self-imaging and self-imagining encouraged by social media such as Facebook profiles and Instagram accounts, let alone online dating apps such as Tinder, all allow users to create and maintain a 'personality' for the benefit of likes and follows. Never is this more evident than in the sheer number of photos of oneself that are available online and in digital format. The word 'selfie' was Oxford dictionary's word of the year in 2013 and its first use can be traced back to Australia in 2002, where it was used in an online forum (Oxford Dictionaries, 2016). Adorno and Benjamin both recognised technologically reproducible products of the culture industry as historical and contextual and thus allowed for the continual evolution of such products.

By reading Adorno alongside Benjamin, and by acknowledging the power of films, media and other products of the culture industry to be potentially constructive (allowing for autonomy) or destructive (fetishising the product for ideological or economic means), we get a more holistic vision of such media as socially situated activity. There is a need to focus on the critical attitude of the spectator and user of such media, as well as the moral messages of the medium. This is particularly apparent when we consider what the majority of consumers willingly ingest uncritically. Adorno and Benjamin both offer a historical account linking their aesthetics to audience reception and experience. Mass art and online media communicate ideas and values that are received by people. While there are many different stories being told in contemporary culture, the focus on the critical thinker, the interpreter of the narrative, is vital.

Adorno's method sometimes appears paradoxical, and his principle of negative dialectics suggests that we know freedom through its negation, and, likewise, autonomy when we are restricted. It is the paradox of knowing what is not an example of freedom or autonomy that allows us to aim at what is and, Osborne points out, these terms are not defined in a positive or epistemic manner. Rather, the terms operate as paradoxes in order for us to work towards liberty and autonomy. Osborne writes, "One cannot simply posit freedom as if it could be unproblematically known: one is better occupied on a more negative task, in diagnosing the forces of unfreedom" (p. 39).

While Adorno worries about Hollywood Studio films, Benjamin focusses more on the avant-garde, the films of Eisenstein. Benjamin's optimism may be partly a result of the artworks with which he engages. Osborne claims,

> Benjamin is diagnosing the progressive or at least redemptive potentiality of modern forms of mass art. Adorno's whole question seems to be quite different from this: to measure the modern culture industry in ultimately ethical terms, that is, in terms of its relation to the forces of critical self-reflection.

Where Adorno sees regression, Benjamin sees possibility; but this is a difference that is the product of their differing critical styles more than anything else.

(p. 62)

Osborne's comparison reveals that Benjamin and Adorno are not using the same
methodology; nor are they offering oppositional arguments. Thus, they both
offer useful ideas to contemporary philosophers and educators. Indeed, Adorno's
critique of Benjamin is useful in offering a subtle re-reading of both. Adorno
laments Benjamin's lack of a dialectical perspective (p. 62). Adorno writes to
Benjamin on 18 March 1936, stating,

> In your earlier writings . . . you distinguished the idea of the work of art as a
> structure from the symbol of theology on the one hand, and from the taboo
> of magic on the other. I now find it somewhat disturbing – and here I can
> see a sublimated remnant of certain Brechtian themes – that you have now
> rather casually transferred the concept of the magical aura to the 'autono-
> mous work of art' and flatly assigned a counter-revolutionary function to
> the latter.
>
> (p. 128)

The question of whether mass artwork and social media are valuable as a tool to
prompt critical thinking becomes tied to the idea that they do, or do not, have
an aura. As seen in Adorno's comment above, the definition of what an aura is
changes and is unclear. Benjamin defines 'aura' as "A strange weave of space and
time: the unique appearance or semblance of distance, no matter how close it
may be" (Benjamin, 1991–1999, pp. 518–519). Deleuze echoes this definition
in the concepts of time and space on which he focusses his cinema books written
in the 1980s. Fredric Jameson calls attention to the dialectic occurring between
Benjamin and Adorno, explaining,

> Riposting against Benjamin's attack on aesthetic 'aura' as a vestige of bour-
> geois culture and his celebration of the progressive function of technologi-
> cal reproducibility in art as the pathway to a new appropriation of it by the
> masses – realized above all in the cinema, Adorno replied with a defence of
> avant-garde art and a counter-attack against over-confidence in commercial-
> popular art.
>
> (Bloch et al., 1977, p. 106)

The letters between Benjamin and Adorno between 1935–1939 reveal much of
the strengths and weaknesses of both writers' theories. The publication of these
letters in English in 1999 invoked resurgence in interest in both scholars, particularly Adorno, who has been somewhat neglected by philosophy of film scholars,
who have been attracted to the more optimistic writings of Benjamin. Adorno
insightfully recognises the 'psychogistic subjectivism and ahistorical romanticism'
in Benjamin's work and notes the Spinozean influence upon Benjamin that could

develop in one of two extreme directions: it can be taken as a primal nostalgia for unity with nature: an unbridled romanticism; or as a utopian vision of classless-ness that lacks class (or 'taste') entirely (Bloch et al., 1977, p. 103). The problem is that both perspectives are ungrounded, floating in a de-contextualised space, not linked to social reality, time and place. In this way, both perspectives become overly subjective and emotive. The critical insight Adorno has into Benjamin's work is one reason we should reconsider his critique of, not only Benjamin's optimism, but the contemporary optimistic approach towards technologically mass-produced and consumed media (Bloch et al., 1977, p. 104). This is not to argue that we should adopt Adorno's negative critique wholesale either, but, in an effort to promote critical engagement with multimedia sources of information and mass artworks, we should critically consider and engage with both Adorno and Benjamin.

For Adorno, the beauty of the work of art *qua* artwork is that it doesn't tie up its ideas neatly and instead challenges the receiver to view reality in its represen-tation, replete with its tensions and discordance. If art allows the viewer to see that there are multiple perspectives, it encourages critical spectatorship. In this way, "art is negative knowledge of the actual world" (1967, p. 32). Adorno here refers to the method of negative dialectics whereby one recognises the paradoxes in society and can thus be a critical or active thinker. If mass art can allow for the same understanding, it fails to be limited to a homogeneous status quo. It would appear that social media may allow for critical engagement by allowing multiple (endless) voices to join in to a conversation, online, in forums or on social media apps such as Twitter, for instance. The irony of social media is that, even while users have endless access to multiple, diverse voices, we usually seek out those reinforcing our own biases and beliefs. This echo-chamber effect is partly respon-sible for what is now labelled a 'post-truth' age in which the feeling or sensation evoked matters more to people than the facts – something that will be further explored in the next chapter.

Conclusion

As philosophers and educators look to how mass art, media and social media can be used, we can consider the critical and celebratory perspectives offered by Adorno and Benjamin as a starting point. Questions of spectatorship, engage-ment and up-take of technologically produced, reproduced and distributed mass objects necessarily invoke ethical concerns and aesthetic judgements. The func-tionality and impact of mass art, media and social media are also worthy of exami-nation given their accessibility and popularity. In reference to film, Badiou is one theorist who claims that this accessibility is a good thing. "After Deleuze," Badiou writes, "there is a courting of philosophy by cinema – or of cinema by philosophy" (Badiou, 2009, p. 1). The massness of cinematic art Badiou ascribes to 'general humanity' and claims is democratic in nature. It is also, of course, economic and technological, political and social. Mass artworks such as films and media may promote a critical response to society, yet it may be that such works are already preaching to the converted. For those texts that do not provoke a critical response, we must consider how to encourage those engaging with such works to be critical, particularly given this includes critiquing the social, political and moral messages latent therein or actively promoted. Again, it is the attitude of critical perspectivism that is of relevance here as this is the attitude that should be adopted when presented with any such values, scenarios and narratives. There are practical implications and ethical concerns that mass untutored audiences, including children, are watching depictions of events or stories that may contain unethical or even harmful messages. Teaching audiences to think critically and respond to others with compassion is vital, particularly when we consider the various technological media such as the broadcast news, the Internet, blogs and other social media platforms.

How the mass-produced and distributed object or media should be valued (aesthetically and ethically), its effect (its impact upon viewers, its critical reception as well as its production, including the intention of the author(s)) are all important issues. Where there is the potential for positive or life-affirming messages or affect being conveyed, there is equally the potential for the transmission of life-denying or nihilistic messages. If mass art and media encourages viewers to critique society, Adorno and Benjamin would claim this is a good thing. However, where passive viewing is promoted, we must ask what values are being uncritically ingested and whether or not this has an effect on viewers and on society. Ultimately I will conclude that we do not necessarily need censorship; rather, we need critical reception and continued dialogue. We need for those engaging with mass art and media objects and social platforms to do so with a critically perspectival attitude. This is of the utmost importance in a world where so much is uncritically ingested and mass messages are transmitted and seductively screened ubiquitously. To paraphrase Adorno, the art will change only when its audiences do. Ideally there will be a growth in ethical consumerism as people become increasingly critically perspectival. Yet this hope relies on education and the habituation of virtuous conduct and ethical choices. In the next chapter, I will explore the attitude of critical perspectivism with respect to multiliteracies and social media before considering educative possibilities in chapter five.[1]

Note

1 This chapter was published in an earlier form as D'Olimpio, L. (2014). Thoughts on film: Critically engaging with both Adorno and Benjamin. *Educational Philosophy and Theory*, 47(6), 622–637. DOI: 10.1080/00131857.2014.964161 reprinted in an altered form here and published with permission of the publisher (Taylor & Francis Ltd, www.tandfonline.com).

References

Adorno, T. W., & Benjamin, W. (1999). *The complete correspondence 1928–1940* (H. Lonitz (Ed.) & N. Walker, trans.). Cambridge: Harvard University Press.

Adorno, T. W., & Horkheimer, M. (1997). The culture industry: Enlightenment as mass deception. In T. W. Adorno & M. Horkheimer (Eds.), *Dialectic of enlightenment*. London: Verso.

Adorno, T. W. (1975). Culture industry reconsidered. *New German Critique*, 6, 12–19.

Adorno, T. W. (1967). *Prisms* (S. Weber & S. Weber, trans.). Cambridge: MIT Press.

Adorno, T. W. (1981–1982). Transparencies on film (T. Y. Levin, trans.). *New German Critique*, Special Double Issue on New German Cinema 24/25, 199–205.

Badiou, A. (2009). Cinema as a democratic emblem (A. Ling & A. Mondon, trans.). *Parrhesia*, 6: 1–6.

Benjamin, W. (1991–1999). *Selected Writings* (H. Eiland & M. W. Jennings, Eds.). Cambridge: Harvard University Press.

Benjamin, W. (1969). The work of art in the age of mechanical reproduction (H. Zorn, trans.). In H. Arendt (Ed.), *Illuminations* (pp. 217–252). New York: Schocken Books.

Brummett, B. (2013). What popular films teach us about values: Locked inside with the Rage Virus. *Journal of Popular Film and Television*, 41(2): 61–67.

Bloch, E. et al., (1977). Aesthetics and politics (R. Taylor, trans.). Radical Thinkers Series. London: Verso.

Carroll, N. (2004). The power of movies. In P. Lamarque & S. H. Olsen (Eds.), *Aesthetics and the philosophy of art: The analytic tradition* (pp. 485–497). Oxford: Blackwell.

Carroll, N. (1998). *A philosophy of mass art*. Oxford: Clarendon Press.

Carroll, N. (1988). Art, practice and narrative. *Monist*, 71(2): 140–156.

Carroll, N. (1994). Identifying art. In R. Yanal (Ed.), *Institutions of art*. University Park: Pennsylvania State University Press.

Carroll, N. (1993). Historical narratives and the philosophy of art. *Journal of Aesthetics and Art Criticism*, 51(3): 313–326.

Chalmers, D. (2016). David Chalmers on Pokémon Go and the future of reality' interviewed on ABC Radio National's 'The Philosopher's Zone'. Retrieved August 19, 2016, from www.abc.net.au/radionational/programs/philosopherszone/david-chalmers-on-pokemon-go-and-the-future-of-reality/7662524. Accompanied by 'The Value of Virtual Worlds' article 1/8/2016, an edited extract from Chalmers' 'The Virtual and the Real'.

Chaplin, C. Dir. (1936). *Modern times*. Film.

Collingwood, R. G. (1969). *The principles of art*. Oxford: Oxford University Press.

Colman, F. (2011). *Deleuze & Cinema: The film concepts*. Oxford: Berg Publishers.

Deleuze, G. (1986). *Cinema I: The movement-image* (H. Tomlinson and B. Habberjam, trans.). Minneapolis: University of Minnesota Press.

Deleuze, G. (1989). *Cinema II: The time-image*. Minneapolis: University of Minnesota Press.

Devereaux, M. (1998). Beauty and evil: The case of Leni Riefenstahl's *Triumph of the Will*. In J. Levinson (Ed.), *Aesthetics and ethics: Essays at the intersection*. New York: Cambridge University Press.

Hansen, M. (1981–1982). Introduction to Adorno, 'Transparencies on Film' (1966). *New German Critique*, Special Double Issue on *New German Cinema*, 24/25, 186–198.

Levine, M. (2001). Depraved spectators & impossible audiences: Horror and other pleasures of the cinema. *Film and Philosophy*, Special Edition on Horror, 5: 63–71.

Levinson, J. (2004). Defining art historically. In P. Lamarque and S. H. Olsen (Eds.), *Aesthetics and the philosophy of art: The analytic tradition*. Oxford: Blackwell.

Markus, G. (2001). Walter Benjamin or: The commodity as Phantasmagoria. *New German Critique, 83*: 3–42.

McCann, P. (2008). *Race, music, and national identity: Images of Jazz in American fiction, 1920–1960*. Delaware: Associated University Press.

Osborne, T. (2008). *The structure of modern cultural theory*. Manchester: Manchester University Press.

Osborne, P., and Charles, M. (2011). Walter Benjamin. In E. N. Zalta (Ed.), *The Stanford encyclopedia of philosophy*. Retrieved from http://plato.stanford.edu/archives/spr2011/entries/benjamin/

Oxford Dictionaries. (2016). Oxford: Oxford University Press. Oxford dictionaries press release. Retrieved September 6, 2016, from http://blog.oxforddictionaries.com/press-releases/oxford-dictionaries-word-of-the-year-2013/

Riefenstahl, L. (1935). Dir. *Triumph of the will*. Film.

The Minefield, ABC Radio National. Radio Interview 14 July 2016. Waleed Aly, Scott Stephens and Laura D'Olimpio. Retrieved September 6, 2016, from www.abc.net.au/radionational/programs/theminefield/first-as-pokemon-then-as-farce/7630046. Supplemented by 'First as Pokémon, Then as Farce? The Risks of the Modern Culture Industry' opinion piece for ABC Religion and Ethics website by L. D'Olimpio (2016). Retrieved from www.abc.net.au/religion/articles/2016/07/14/4500332.htm

Wartenberg, T. E. (2007). *Thinking on screen: Film as philosophy*. London: Routledge.

Wartenberg, T. E. (2006). Beyond mere illustration: How films can be philosophy. *The Journal of Aesthetics and Art Criticism, 64*(1), 19–32.

Weitz, M. (2004). The role of theory in aesthetics. In P. Lamarque and S. H. Olsen (Eds.), *Aesthetics and the philosophy of art: The analytic tradition*. Oxford: Blackwell.

4 Social media and multiliteracies

Multiliteracies are contemporary skills sorely needed in the current technological age. Multiliteracies is a term coined by the New London Group when they first met in September 1994 because "it describes two important arguments we might have with the emerging cultural, institutional, and global order. The first argument engages with the multiplicity of communications channels and media; the second with the increasing salience of cultural and linguistic diversity" (Cope & Kalantzis, 2000, p. 5). The term is useful because it "supplements traditional literacy pedagogy" and acknowledges the features of representation that go beyond language in order to include culture and context (Cope & Kalantzis, 2000, p. 5). While it may be the case that we now need a "new New London Group" (Gee, 2009, p. 196), given the digital revolution, I make use of the word here because, like the members of the original New London Group, the term reflects the fact that literacy is multiple. As such, literacy is "embedded in multiple socially and culturally constructed practices" rather than as a "uniform set of mental abilities or processes" (Gee, 2009, p. 196). In order to engage well with multiliteracies, one must adopt a critical and moral disposition flexible enough to take into account the variety of contexts and perspectives presented by a range of media. I argue that the appropriate attitude to achieve such ethical engagement is critical perspectivism as I have herein detailed.

In the face of our ubiquitous use of mass art, media and social media, people need to learn how to use such tools critically and ethically if participation in society is to be democratic and fair. Democratic in this sense refers to truly listening to diverse voices even while recognising a common humanity amongst contextual and individual difference. Ethical here refers to treating others with compassion while maintaining a respect for truth and knowledge based on sound evidence. Seeking truth in the face of such multiplicity may sound naively optimistic or idealistic, or downright old fashioned. Yet it is still the case that the human experience is one with common shared elements, even more so as the global world is more connected than ever previously and the language of images prevalent in the media cut across nationalistic and geographical boundaries. As existential threats unite us in fear of the implications of climate change and extremist factions, the antidote to negative news and clickbait media is a moderate approach to relaying information that reminds us of our connectedness and common humanity. We must remember how to listen to one another and reasonably disagree in public and private spaces, while also seeking solutions to problems that affect us all. The skills of communication, rational argumentation, critical assessment of arguments and the willingness to build upon, as opposed to solely tearing down, one another's ideas are important, transferable skills that can be used face-to-face or online. Such skills need to be taught from an early age and then practiced until they become habitual expressions of our respect for others. They must also be supported by appropriate emotional dispositions such as care and compassion. It is these skills that will enable people to adopt the attitude of critical perspectivism and apply it to their engagement with art, mass art, media, and online sources of information and entertainment.

Having explored how literature and other narrative artworks such as film require us to be critically as well as compassionately engaged, while also potentially encouraging viewers to adopt such an ethical perspective, this chapter will focus on examples of social media. Examples will be investigated to see how critical perspectivism supports an ethical engagement with social media, and it shall become clear that this moral attitude is precisely what is required in a digital age of multiliteracies. A critical eye, when supplemented by a caring disposition, is akin to a critically perspectival approach that should be adopted when engaging with Web 2.0.

Today's Web 2.0 allows for increased engagement and participation as users create as well as interact with and respond to content. This differs from the World Wide Web (WWW, or what has retrospectively been termed Web 1.0) for which content was mostly curated. Web 2.0, a buzzword introduced around 2003–2004, and the accompanying social media platforms, wikis, blogs and networking sites ensure that online spaces are dynamic and inclusive. Web 2.0 is characterised by unique features due to its technological nature and digital storytelling, which opens up new ways of telling stories, including accelerating the pace of creation and participation while discovering new directions in which narratives can flow.

Two essential features that make Web 2.0 projects and platforms distinct include microcontent and social media (Alexander & Levine, 2008, p. 41). Microcontent is when authors each create a small 'chunk' of content focussed on a single idea or concept and these can overlap. Examples of microcontent include blog posts, wiki edits, YouTube comments, and images, photos, gifs, or videos. The second feature unique to Web 2.0 is social software, more commonly referred to as social media. Social media allows for sharing and commenting on microcontent via sharing platforms that are housed at a URL site and can boast a guest book or members and searchable categories. For example, Flickr, Instagram, Facebook, Twitter and Snapchat are social media platforms which use hashtags, 'friends' or followers and groups to assist users to identify microcontent along thematic lines and thus join in the conversation on a particular topic or add additional microcontent to a thread, or simply see what their friends are posting and commenting on. In this online space, readers become storytellers by adding information or microcontent into the digital narrative and expanding upon it, allowing it to spin off into other forms or across various social media sites. Often certain instances of such phenomena will then be picked up and discussed further offline via regular media platforms such as radio and television (most of which will have corresponding social media profiles and/or handles). In this way, something that started as a social media update by an ordinary citizen may end up being reported on news pages, panel discussion shows, podcasts or radio programs, only to eventually be discussed face-to-face by strangers at the water cooler at work or in the school playground. It is in this way the democratic space of Web 2.0 allows for expansive storytelling that can have an unexpected impact in the world.

Web 2.0 is equitable in allowing low-barrier access to information along with the tools and technology that enable almost anyone to communicate with almost anyone else, while also opening up a truly global market space for ideas, content, products and services. Unusually, the voice of the consumer or user is more immediate and responsive than anything seen previously, and the resulting barrage of opinions and reviews can drown out the voices of experts. This democratisation of the Internet is marked by users including individuals as well as groups, institutions, companies and governments. Such accessibility has supported and in turn been supported by neoliberal policies which advocate corporate deregulation, privatisation, competition, entrepreneurialism, and open markets to achieve both financial success and individual self-creation. Marwick notes that, "while these policies have met with global protests, they have become the predominant paradigm of the twenty-first century" (2013, p. 11). Any account of the role the media and mass-produced and distributed art and entertainment objects may play in society must take into account the concerns of how the neoliberal and consumerist agenda monetises every technological interaction.

In 1964, Marshall McLuhan published *Understanding Media: The Extensions of Man*, in which he spoke about the media as an extension of ourselves. Never is this more apparent than today. Users of Web 2.0 constantly create and re-create themselves using avatars, images and symbolic actions. The ease and speed at which this now occurs is startling, enabled by the mobile technology that sees smartphones being carried around with people everywhere they go. In fact, these mobile technologies are often felt to be an important part of a user's identity, and it is common to hear people say that they feel as though they have 'lost an arm' when they do not have their smartphone on their person or within easy reach. With Clark and Chalmers (1998) defending an extended mind hypothesis, it could be claimed that the smartphone is actually an extension of one's consciousness or memory. Granted, the question as to whether my notebook computer (their example) is a part of my memory is said to be a puzzle on their account (p. 17), yet Clark and Chalmers acknowledge that some crucial (necessary) criteria for extended belief are shared by their theory and the way the person attached to the smart phone (or notebook) uses this technological tool which contains all of one's information and connects them to others. Even if we do not wish to apply the extended mind hypothesis to our smart devices, we can see the ever-increasing role such technology plays in our lives.

Meanwhile, McLuhan saw language as a medium or technology, paving the way for our understanding of multiliteracies as new languages that non-digital natives must learn to speak, even as digital natives grow up surrounded by these new literacies. Certainly there is still an important role for education in assisting us to learn how to use these literacies well, in a way that contributes constructively rather than destructively to our lives. This is a role schools have been slow to take up, struggling to keep up with the rapid rate of technological advancements. McLuhan wisely noted that "our new electric technology that extends our senses and nerves in a global embrace has large implications for the future of language" (1995, p. 80). As we increasingly move from a language of words and listening to a language of images and seeing, encouraged by Web 2.0, we witness the birth of a universal language. The universal language of images, however, is limited and easily misinterpreted when words and contextual understanding are restricted and, in a digital age, tone minimised (even when taking into account emoticons and emojis).

With respect to Web 2.0, one central concern is the idea that, when communication is technologically mediated, people sometimes forget that they are interacting with real-life others. This is where the idea of compassion becomes of paramount importance. It is not simply critical, analytical and rational thinking skills that good citizens need to possess, it is also rational emotions such as compassionate and the ability to work and play in a collaborative setting alongside others. Therefore, while there is certainly the need for critical discernment when sorting through the information and misinformation abundant online, there is also the need to respect others as thinking *and feeling* human beings. It is particularly obvious online in a global, decontextualised space that we need to accommodate pluralism in the sense that we will discover multiple perspectives and conflicting attitudes amongst people. However, we must also recognise the normative aspect of shared human values and virtues that are common to all. Ultimately, everyone wishes to be free to do what they wish to do and not to have that freedom thwarted or unfairly infringed. This basic recognition of the fact that others are more similar to us than they are different results in a fundamental moral principle such as the 'golden rule', where we do not do to others what we would not have them to do to us. This guiding ethical principle can work quite well in support of a democratic and harmonious community when applied to how we treat others online or face-to-face.

Yet the golden rule may not be immediately obvious or easy to apply in practice, and for this reason we must consider educative or formative possibilities which allow for the modelling, teaching and habituation of compassionate responses, particularly towards others whose beliefs differ from one's own. Furthermore, when considering the impact of globalisation on curriculum and pedagogy, educationalists face two main concerns. Firstly, how to teach learners to be global consumers or citizens. This includes a focus on global values, social justice, sustainable development and environmental education (Edwards & Usher, 2008, p. 53). Secondly, the impact of informational technologies and the emergence of global education as a result of such technology. But at the risk that these two focal points are considered all-encompassing, we must not forget the interaction between the global, the local and the regional. There is not one hegemonic voice emerging alongside globalisation, and certainly not in the context of the neoliberal agenda (Edwards & Usher, 2008, p. 53). Educational spaces are no longer closed and fixed in an Internet age, particularly with the emergence of Web 2.0, and the teacher is no longer the sole, authoritative source of meaning. This is the case across all schooling levels, from primary to secondary to tertiary. Multimodality and media allow for a range of interpretations to be more visible and accessible than ever previously, and this is echoed in the way we now speak of meaning-making, rather than 'meaning', as participants interact in order to jointly construct and co-construct meaning.

This new participatory mode of engagement can be viewed optimistically as power relations shift and democratic access to information is abundant amidst the global connectivity of Web 2.0. In fact, Cunningham et al. claim that the incorporation of Information and Communication Technologies (ICTs) and associated modes of communication into pedagogies are more likely to encourage independent life-long learning skills and we are more aware than ever before of the 'bigger picture'. They are "optimistic about the potential of global technologies to create information democracy and low cost access to a whole range of knowledges" (Cunningham et al., 1997, p. 160, quoted in Edwards & Usher, 2008, p. 65). This new mode of learning challenges the original notion of reciprocity as multiple paths of nonlinear teaching and learning interactions open up (Edwards & Usher, 2008, p. 55). Such nonlinear educational possibilities include those formed between teachers and students, students and students, teachers and teachers, as well as the wider community. Such possibilities always existed, yet they are certainly enhanced by the technological tools we now have at our disposal.

However, Edwards & Usher (2008) rightly point out that, while virtual communities may well have democratising potential, they are not inherently democratic themselves, and, even if they were, whether or not this would translate into the classroom or physically embodied social spaces is another question worthy of investigation. Furthermore, even though online spaces are participatory, not all forms of participation are democratic. They write:

> it is clear then that what is involved here is not just a straightforward matter of bringing in democracy by deploying new technologies. Although a decentred and interactive classroom experience can have potentially democratic effects, whether these will still be present depends on the wider social context. Cyberspace produces new formations of social and economic power and it is against these that its democratic actuality must be judged.
>
> (p. 65)

McAfee is also keen to remind us that any political engagement online is still situated in a real-world context. It is simply not the case that the Internet is a different world, even if it is a decontextualised space. The political system, she argues, "is embedded within a larger life world, especially in an era of networked public spheres" (2015, p. 274).

As McAfee notes, new media gives us a powerful political tool: a tool that allows us to be creative and attend to multiple things at once. At the same time, the public sphere is wider than ever previously, and we can engage in political life in new and interesting ways. There is a public visibility and transparency in our ability to see analytics, statistics and the numbers of likes, shares and comments on social media. Web 2.0 can be used to quickly raise awareness of causes or unethical behaviour, and encourage a swift and widespread backlash or support in favour of or against specific actions or utterances. Yet this also gives rise to slacktivism and a laziness that equates clicking 'like' with having democratically participated in a meaningful collective action that has political import. As we saw with other narrative artworks and mass art examples explored previously, the medium itself may be ethically neutral, yet how it is used is central to our debate.

Even if we focus on the use of the media, it must also be acknowledged that the in-built limitations of such media will support and encourage a particular mode of communication and interaction. With many social media platforms, utterances use images more than words, and quick responses, likes and shares are encouraged. As a result, online debates may be frustrating in their lack of sensitivity and nuance, in which ideas are decontextualised and short, snappy, click-bait headlines are constructed in order to grab one's attention in an overcrowded space. McAfee notes that "these public conversations and deliberations can be, however, so fragmented, decentred, and often fractious that it is hard to discern them collectively as democratic" (2015, p. 289). Furthermore, apps and social networking sites themselves are treating people as consumers rather than as citizens. The shifting privacy policies, the selling of data to advertising companies so that they may better target personalised advertisements, not to mention the widespread social experiments conducted by Facebook without users' knowledge or consent is all indicative of the loss of autonomy and privacy that accompanies our desire to be connected and informed.

Never has this interconnectivity been more evident to the world than in the wake of the 2016 US Election that saw Donald Trump sworn in as President on 20 January 2017, and the Brexit Referendum that saw the UK vote to leave the European Union. Social media played a larger role in public decision making and voting than ever previously as evidenced by previously reliable exit polls being unable to fully account for and predict the majority public opinion. Some of the worry with respect to the use of social media is that public figures and politicians may rally the general public to their cause through charisma and by being emblematic rather than persuading people through an appeal to facts. Web 2.0 spreads rumours and misinformation as quickly as it spreads news, and, in light of 'truthiness', 'fake news', and 'alternative facts' it seems as though democratic participation in society is under threat when democracies rely on voters being well informed and able to support policies that enhance the common good. While Web 2.0 can assist people to access information, it also provides a forum for the creation of echo-chambers whereby individuals seek only to reinforce their previous biases and myths. This contemporary feature of the technologically mediated society is summed up by The Oxford Dictionaries Word of the Year for 2016:

'post-truth'; an adjective defined as 'relating to or denoting circumstances in which objective facts are less influential in shaping public opinion than appeals to emotion and personal belief.'

Importantly, public media 2.0 looks and functions differently to media of the past in that it is both for and by the public, and is democratic in this way. Yet this does not occur by accident, or for free (McAfee, 2015, p. 290). McAfee notes, "the idea that citizens can, through public and other participatory media, make worlds together does not mean that people will be united and "civil". On the contrary, there will be vigorous disagreements. But the tenor of discourse changes when people realise that you and I have to figure out a way to go forward" (2015, p. 291). The only way people will be civil online is if they are generally civil. The only way people will use technological tools democratically is if they are already committed to being democratic and inclusive. Such attitudes, including reasonableness and compassion, must be trained initially *as well as* be supported in society, by policies and institutions, corporations and governments, both face-to-face and online.

In this chapter, I will provide some examples of the perils and pitfalls of social media that may be classified as hoaxes, scams and catfishing. I will offer suggestions as to how we can educate people to avoid and be protected against such hoaxes and scams, even while still maintaining a compassionate disposition towards others with whom one communicates online. I will apply the attitude of critical perspectivism to each case study to see if it stands up to the test that allows the person adopting this attitude to be mindful, ethical and critically reflective when dealing with or confronted with such examples. I will conclude that these transferable thinking skills are ones we've always had to use for as long as human societies have contained tricksters, cheats, larrikins, and criminals. Yet I also note the specific features inherent in the technological nature of social networking sites, social media, the Internet and Web 2.0 that give a particular character and new angle to these classic dangers. Even if the hoaxes or scams themselves are not particularly frightening or threatening, the nature of the media that encourages speed of reply and immediate interaction may make users more vulnerable to accidentally stumbling into such traps. Thus, teachers, parents, citizens and young people themselves must seek to be critically perspectival when playing, working, or networking online, and we must find ways to educate our young people as to the best way to do this. One good way to educate young people to be savvy online is by using real life or fictional examples and case studies in the classroom that can be discussed and critiqued. The teacher is likely to learn as much from this exercise and ensuing dialogue as the students.

Hoaxes and scams

A hoax is a humorous or malicious deception, a trick, or a plan to deceive someone. A scam is an illegal plan for making money, especially one that involves tricking people. To debunk is to show that something is less important, less good, or less true than it has been made to appear (definitions from the online Cambridge

Dictionary). There are several well-respected online sources, including Hoax-Slayer and Snopes.com, dedicated to exposing hoaxes and scams, debunking myths and halting the dissemination of false information. Hoax-Slayer, created by Australian Brett Christensen has been, as espoused on the website, 'debunking hoaxes and exposing scams since 2003!' and is archived as an online resource by the National Library of Australia.

On Hoax-Slayer's often updated list of top ten scams (stories that users have most read and shared) are scams that involve a promise that if you 'click here' you can get a free voucher from Marks & Spencer. This scam is not associated in any way with the UK retailer, and no voucher will be forthcoming. The trick is aimed at encouraging victims to divulge personal details on so-called survey websites, allowing the perpetrators of the scam to then use the victim's personal details in a phishing scheme. Another 'popular' scam is the 'stalker' app that encourages you to download and install an app allowing you to check who has been viewing your Facebook (or other social media) profile online. These 'See Who Viewed Your Profile' scams are often posted on the social media site itself, such as Facebook, and again are designed to direct the user to a spam survey website, possibly encouraging them to sign up to an expensive mobile phone text messaging service, and sharing their personal details with the scammers.

Another website that has gained International renown for debunking myths, rumours and dispelling misinformation is Snopes.com with the by-line "rumor has it" Created by American couple Barbara and David Mikkelson, and also referred to as the 'Urban Legends Reference Page', Snopes.com seeks the truth about urban legends, questionable emails and rumours and other stories of debatable truth or questionable origin. The website welcomes users to "the definitive Internet reference source for urban legends, folklore, myths, rumors, and misinformation" and features fact checks, news stories and a top 25 of urban legends. What is epistemically interesting is how much of a need there is for such services and the proliferation and recurrence of hoaxes, scams and fake news. These stories and tricks can be spread extremely quickly, going 'viral' in a matter of hours, via social media sources that connect a worldwide audience.

Apart from fake news and rumours, snopes.com advises of common scams that can affect people, particularly if the victims are suffering financial distress. Such scams often employ a 'generic' story lacking details, and use an emotional hook along with a time sensitivity clause to encourage a quick, emotional response from their victims. From their website, the 'top scams' listed include:

Nigerian scam

A wealthy foreigner who needs help moving millions of dollars from his homeland promises a hefty percentage of this fortune as a reward for assisting him.

Foreign lottery scam

Announcements inform recipients that they've won large sums of money in foreign lotteries.

Secret shopper scam

Advertisers seek applicants for paid positions as 'secret' or 'mystery' shoppers.

Work-at-home scam

Advertisers offer kits that enable home workers to make money posting links on the Internet.

Family member in distress scam

Scammers impersonate distressed family members in desperate need of money.

Some government authorities have set up websites such as Australia's "Scamwatch" set up by the Australian Competition and Consumer Commission that includes real-life stories of people who have been duped by scams, advice for avoiding scams (for individuals or businesses) and statistics. In Australia in 2016, there were 144 433 reports of various scams, which resulted in $77 123 877 loss to victims, although this figure only pertains to 7.2% of the reports. The overwhelming majority of the reported scams that resulted in financial loss pertained to 'dating and romance', with the second highest category classified as 'phishing', which the website describes as 'attempts by scammers to trick you into giving out personal information such as your bank account numbers, passwords and credit card numbers'. The main method scammers use to lure their victims is the telephone (57 893 reports in Australia in 2016 resulting in a loss of $21 734 609), the Internet (11 027 reports in Australia in 2016 resulting in a loss of $19 473 744), and via email (48 442 reports in Australia in 2016 resulting in a loss of $16 805 473), with social media listed as the fourth likely delivery method (4 380 reports in Australia in 2016 resulting in a loss of $8 601 057), with the overwhelming majority of victims aged 40+. These statistics demonstrate that it is not just young school-aged people who need to be trained to be critical when engaging with others; older generations who are not digital natives are actually more at risk of being tricked or conned out of their savings.

In most of these scams, being compassionate is not going to protect you from being conned or tricked. In fact, quite the opposite. These scammers prey upon qualities of generosity, sympathy, desperation as well as greed in order to hook their victims. This is where sympathetically engaging with the story of the other is not the ideal method for dealing with emails that are sent into your inbox purporting to be from someone you know. Critical thinking and calm, rational consideration is crucial in such instances, along with taking some time to investigate further if you are tempted to worry about the contents of the scam.

One philosophically interesting aspect to these scams is the epistemic criteria that may or may not be invoked in harmless hoaxes. An example of confusion surrounding which epistemic evidence should be relied upon occurred on Facebook a few years ago centred on a joke and giraffe images. Facebook users started to change their profile pictures to an image of a giraffe. There was an accompanying joke that, if you didn't answer correctly, you were told you had to change your Facebook profile picture to an image of a giraffe for three days. At the same time, a message started circulating rapidly on Facebook that claimed that changing your profile picture to that of a giraffe would allow hackers to steal your Facebook login details and remotely control your computer due to the weakness in JPEG images of giraffes. It turns out that the warning message was the actual hoax, not the joke itself. But, as such multi-level tricks unfold, how do we know which message to trust?

For the sake of the example, here is the message that accompanies the joke. This message was circulated as people who got the answer to the riddle wrong were changing their profile pictures to giraffe images (courtesy of snopes.com):

URGENT GIRAFFE GAME NOTICE **URGENT**

Whoah! Just found out that the Giraffe challenge was set up by the hacking group Anonymous. Apparently they're going to embark on a random "cleansing" program which will wipe out the bank accounts and hard drives of those people who have giraffe profile pics . . . A few of my mates already had it happen, so gets to changing your pics back!!! Microsoft and google are working on it now. We recommend Facebook users: DO NOT change your profile picture to giraffes.

What was labelled as 'The Great Giraffe Challenge' of 2013–2014 was simply a harmless game. The accompanying warning message was itself false and highly unlikely to result in any phishing scam victims. The hoax slayers and scam detectors reassured users that no virus lurked in the JPEG based images of giraffes and the possible source of this joke or trick may have been a vulnerability associated with JPEG images viewed via Microsoft Windows back in 2004, which was fixed via a patch released by Microsoft in mid-September of that same year. Even then, the vulnerability was not attached to a particular JPEG image (such as a giraffe), and thus this story was simply a borrowed hook to worry those Facebook users who were altering their profile pictures in response to unsuccessfully answering the riddle. In these instances, checking resources such as Hoax Slayer and Snopes.com is the best source of trusted evidence for basing your belief on what to trust. In such cases an appeal to a relevant authority seems sensible and prudent.

Critically perspectival users of social media may not, by themselves, always be able to discern which message to trust. A degree of caution and scepticism online is advisable, which may result in users of social media being slow to play a game, participate in a fad, or try a new app because they take the time to firstly investigate whether or not the game or fad is a hoax or a trick or the app in question is safe, reliable and user-friendly. This will often involve looking for further information beyond the social media platform in question. One must always consider how epistemically reliable the information one is accessing is according to the criteria of justified true belief. Critical thinkers will consider the source of the information, and will examine the website(s) they are accessing for tell-tale signs of credibility. Such signs will include the certifications and symbols of authentication, as well as an 'about' or 'contact information' section that depicts a real place and/or email address which can be Googled. When it comes to hoaxes and scams, the trick is to remember to take the time to check the evidence and the epistemic criteria before reacting quickly and emotionally. In such cases, it is reacting either with frantic worry or a complete lack of fear that may make a user susceptible to falling victim to a hoax or scam. Checking whether or not you should believe what you are being told is vitally important and will protect you more than any urge to send your long lost cousin who is supposedly suddenly and unexpectedly visiting Nigeria some money in order to help them return home. The critically perspectival user of social media will pause and reflect on what they are doing prior to engaging with online games, fads, or dubious apps that appeal to base emotions such as envy or greed.

Catfishing

More worrying in its maliciousness and its propensity to prey upon well-intentioned victims' hopes for love, connection and relationship is catfishing. The term was popularised in the 2010 documentary *Catfish*, and refers to scams involving the creation of fictional online personas that are then used to manipulate people and lure victims into what they take to be authentic or genuine communication. The tag-line of the documentary is 'Don't let anyone tell you what it is' and sees the two young filmmakers (directors Henry Joost and Ariel Schulman) document their colleague's budding online friendship with a young woman and her family. Significantly, the woman in question turns out to be unlike the depicted representation on her social media profile. Given the majority of successful scams that resulted in financial loss in Australia last year were classified as dating and romance scams, catfishing obviously works. Furthermore, it is not solely financial distress that is caused by victims who fall for such scams; psychological and emotional distress, including feelings of shame, are further negative consequences that can befall those who engage in such communication and get caught up in the scammers trap.

There seems to be something important about these examples, particularly of catfishing, that speaks to the vulnerability of people who respond emotionally to scams. It seems to be the people most desperate to connect with others who are at most risk of being tricked. In this way, it is the very features that make people evolutionarily successful that work against them in such cases because we have evolved to be community-minded and work collaboratively in groups to ensure our survival. It is a willingness to trust others and believe what they say that makes one susceptible to being tricked. Yet there is some research within the field of psychology that links evidence of education (or lack thereof), trust (or lack thereof), and even mood to how gullible one is, and therefore may be used to predict how likely one is to fall prey to a prank, trick or scam (Forgas, 2007; Forgas & East, 2008).

Summing up some of this research, Forgas (2017), citing Kahneman (2011), writes as follows for *The Conversation* on the eve of April's Fool's Day:

> Gullibility occurs because we have evolved to deal with information using two fundamentally different systems, according to Nobel Prize winning psychologist Daniel Kahneman.
>
> > System 1 thinking is fast, automatic, intuitive, uncritical and promotes accepting anecdotal and personal information as true. This was a useful and adaptive processing strategy in our ancestral environment of small, face-to-face groups, where trust was based on life-long relationships. However, this kind of thinking can be dangerous in the anonymous online world.
> > System 2 thinking is a much more recent human achievement; it is slow, analytical, rational and effortful, and leads to the thorough evaluation of incoming information.

Human beings all use both intuitive (system 1) and analytic (system 2) thinking. However, it is analytic thinking that is going to be relevant and important to critical perspectivism. It is analytic thinking that allows us to be critically engaged with what we see, hear and feel. Forgas notes that if we are less trusting, or in a negative mood, we are also more likely to be critical and engage our analytic thinking. However, there are important pro-social benefits to trusting others and seeking to establish and maintain a trusting society or online community (see D'Olimpio, 2016 and 2015 for a fuller discussion on the importance of trust as a virtue that should be cultivated and educated). Importantly, education also reduces gullibility (Preece & Baxter, 2000).

Educating people to critically engage with the ideas, stories and images they are receiving in the world, including online, is the best protection again scams, tricks and hoaxes. When it comes to how critical perspectivism can assist the potential victim to avoid being scammed, it becomes clear that the critically perspectival person must know when to be more critical and when to be more compassionate, even when both responses may be required. The appropriate response will be context-dependent, taking care to consider the epistemic and ethical features of the scenario, and deciding, on balance, what is the best (most prudent) response. In this way, we can see that knowing that one must be critical and knowing that one must be compassionate is only a small part of being critically perspectival. To adopt this attitude successfully, the moral agent must also know how best to employ their critically perspectival judgement and this takes practice. (More will be said about providing opportunities for people to practice being critically perspectival in educational spaces and public spaces in the next two chapters). In this way, critical perspectivism is an ethical attitude that sees compassion or care being balanced alongside and held in check, supported, and applied appropriately by critical reasoning and a consideration of the potential multiple points of view one may take on any given piece of information, story, email or message.

So far, we have considered the potential dangers, harm and pitfalls of scams, tricks and hoaxes, including catfishing and phishing. I now wish to consider the potential of Web 2.0 technologies to raise public awareness about issues and causes, to stimulate and encourage heartwarming responses to others, while also considering the downside and potential backlash to these same instances.

Slacktivism

Social media can raise awareness about important topics and help individuals to feel connected to a global community. Yet the use of social media in highlighting or raising awareness for certain causes may also amount to slacktivism. Slacktivism involves activity that makes use of the Internet to support social or political causes in such a way that does not require much effort, for instance, creating and sign-ing online petitions. Such forms of advocacy, particularly those related to social media, are often derisively referred to as "slacktivism" or "armchair activism". (definition from the online Cambridge Dictionary). The Armchair Activist may simply copy-paste a status update to their social media profile and feel as though they have done *something* to raise awareness for a certain cause, but they may be simply *appearing* to be doing something, particularly if the action performed is unlikely to have any positive impact. One example of this is when people change their profile pictures to a particular politicised image or symbol, or share a certain Twitter hashtag or video that then goes viral but does not result in any tangible beneficial outcome. In such cases, this 'awareness raising' may be harmless, but it also may be ineffectual. This is not to say that slacktivism is always ineffectual, and ultimately it depends on how social media is used in aid of particular causes as to whether the cause is benefitted or awareness is raised.

When it comes to slacktivism, it is not the media platform that is inherently helpful or unhelpful, good or bad; such judgements may be made according to how the media platform is used by individuals in particular instances. Again, as is the case with other media, the critically perspectival user of social media may be able to raise awareness for a cause or encourage donations to a charity by dis-seminating the information widely in an engaging manner online. The critically perspectival online activist will realise that simply posting a photo of themselves 'wearing no make-up' or changing their profile picture to an image of a super-hero is not going to raise awareness or funds for childhood cancer, for instance. However, if there is a fun fad that can be accompanied by a tangible action, such as accompanying the image with a charitable donation, or participating in a fundraising event, then this will have a beneficial impact. Each instance of online slacktivism can thus be assessed as to whether it amounts to activism or not. The armchair activist may have a good intention and feel compassion for others who are suffering, but unless such compassion is accompanied by a critical attitude which enables the slacktivist to reflect upon what might actually help, the sympa-thetic feeling alone is unlikely to result in an action that actually does any good.

Furthermore, there is also the risk of widely disseminating misinformation if the trends that grow in popularity are ill conceived or based on a lack of information.

This can easily occur when many of the people joining in on a certain social media trend lack awareness of the historical circumstances and complexities of the specific debate at hand (for example, see #Kony2012 blogged about at Scientific American). In such instances, critical perspectivism is vitally important. As was noted in relation to other kinds of hoaxes and scams, one must be cautious and appropriately sceptical before liking and sharing the trending video or image that is popular at any given time. Before passing along any information that has gone viral, the critically perspectival user of social media will pause to reflect and investigate whether or not the video or image in question is sincere and epistemically reliable rather than a hoax or a trick. Again, this will often involve looking for further information outside of social media platforms, for example by checking reputable debunking websites.

Having noted that online activism may amount to ineffectual slacktivism, it must also be acknowledged that online activists may promote a positive response to events that boosts morale, encourages ethical awareness and results in moral actions. Social media can be used to set an example of a compassionate response to others in the face of fear and tragedy. An example of the positive use of social media as a form of moral activism can be seen in response to the Sydney Siege of 2014 that occurred at the Lindt Chocolate Café in Martin Place in the city's centre. Even as news of the terrible event unfolded, the Twitter hashtag #IllRide-WithYou went viral, quickly garnering International praise for demonstrating that ordinary, everyday Australians could respond to the threat of terror, violence and racism with an outpouring of compassion and a recognition of common humanity. As reported in *The Atlantic*:

> Monday's hostage crisis in Sydney, Australia may be over, but the circumstances surrounding the incident – in which three people, including the gunman, died and four others were injured following a 16-hour standoff – remain murky. Little is known about the motives of Man Monis, the suspect in the episode, or the details of the police operation that ended the crisis.
>
> It was amid this prevailing uncertainty that a backlash against Australian Muslims started online. As reports spread quickly about the hostage situation – including the religious identity and nationality of the gunman, as well as the involvement of a black flag with the words of the shehada, the Muslim affirmation of faith, on it – the primary hashtag for the episode on Twitter, #SydneySiege, came to embody the occasional and predictable ugliness of the Internet. Xenophobic and anti-Muslim tweets went out and the Australian Defence League, an ultra-right-wing group, threatened confrontations in the Muslim-majority Sydney suburb of Lakemba.

In the wake of such racial profiling and the vilification of Australian Muslims wearing traditional headdresses, some Muslim women removed their hijabs in order to be able to travel peacefully on public transport. A passenger on a train in Brisbane reported seeing a Muslim woman removing her hijab, ostensibly out of fear of being the target of negative commentary or actions. This passenger told her to put it back on and offered to walk with her in solidarity. Upon hearing of this story via Facebook, Sydney TV content editor Tessa Kum, Twitter handle @ sirtessa, was moved and posted to Twitter the bus route she usually took along with an offer to ride with any Muslims who wanted company. In an effort to come up with a Twitter hashtag for other users to do the same, #IllRideWithYou was started, gaining momentum and going viral after being used in almost 120 000 tweets within hours. This example of an outpouring of compassion was heartwarming as it accompanied the broadcast news coverage reporting on the fear and facts of the hostage situation playing out December 15–16 2014.

By adopting an attitude of critical perspectivism, people are able to consider a point of view that is not their own when deciding how they should react or respond to a situation. In the example given above, Tessa Kum and others were able to empathise with Muslim women who may have felt uncomfortable travelling alone and a tangible form of assistance was offered to strangers who needed it. On a larger scale, the people who joined in to support the #IllRideWithYou hashtag were empathising with Muslims who were being discriminated against. This online action, which might otherwise be deemed slacktivism, had a corresponding practical benefit that saw ordinary people refuse to give in to terror and refuse to encourage discrimination. In this way the action represented an offering of civic friendship that allowed for inclusivity at a time when fearful responses threatened to see certain others as worthy of exclusion. Recognising common humanity can motivate an ethical response to a situation and that response may involve a spontaneous outpouring of compassion that is steadily guided by a rational, pragmatic approach. What the #IllRideWithYou response exemplified was a useful, situated reaction to others that are different to oneself and yet recognised as one's neighbours and fellow citizens. It is this ethical response that is both critical and compassionate that is epitomised by an attitude of critical perspectivism.

Conclusion

We seek out information online and we stumble across it. In learning to distinguish between valuable sources of reliable information and the plethora of dross, it is vital that we teach those who engage with such mediums the ability to critically discern between them. This discernment includes being mindful of the assumptions, biases and agendas shaping the reporting of specific stories, facts, and data. When seeing a story online, it is worth checking who is reporting the story, how they are doing so, from where are they getting their facts, and where are they publishing (or reproducing) this information. When such stories, videos and images are shared via social media, it is also important to note the inbuilt limitations of these platforms. While democratic, online activism is different to physical activism in some important respects. It is true that spreading a message via social media allows it to travel globally rapidly, yet online discussion is usually non-instantaneous, asynchronistic, and relativistic. Important non-verbal cues may be lost online and expression may be limited by emoticons, emojis, text-speak or other features of the platform (for example, Twitter limits each tweet to 140 characters plus a link). In these ways, social media is not the best forum to convey a complex political or ethical argument. And yet the power of opinions on social media to persuade others (including large businesses and governments) and to disseminate ideas is undisputed. Even so, we must be mindful that not all opinions should be weighed equally, as some are backed up and reinforced by better evidence and expertise than others. It may be difficult to hear the voices of the experts amongst the cacophony online. Ultimately, online activism may be taken up and further pursued offline and it is precisely due to the power and impact of social media that we need to train users to be critically as well as compassionately engaged with it.

The virtual public sphere is open in an exciting new way with ideas being discussed and debated in a transparent and engaging manner. Yet the openness of the Internet also makes it a public forum that evokes criticism and trolling. Scammers may make use of the open forum to try to trick or scam unsuspecting victims and lure users into a trap that involves a hoax, scam, phishing or catfishing. The technological tools themselves are value-neutral; it is the character that employs them for constructive or destructive means which may be labelled virtuous or vicious. Social media and networking sites may alter with new technological developments, yet it is the individuals using such mediums that requires the focus of educators. At worst, unstructured discussion online is full of misinformation and promotes superstition and anti-scientism. Social media may allow for negative personal attacks or bullying. At best it fosters genuine learning through expansive dialogue that respects those engaging in the discussion and encourages self-reflection. To foster the latter, we must support, promote, model and train the intellectual and moral habits of the individual that includes critical thinking, discernment and compassion. In the next chapter, I will explore how education, and specifically teaching philosophy in schools using the community of inquiry pedagogy, may assist in teaching students to adopt an attitude of critical perspectivism. Instead of dealing with concerns about social media networking sites by banning their use, although arguments in favour of censorship may be appropriate in specific instances, we ought to teach our students to engage critically with information sources, ideas and stories. This critical engagement must be accompanied by a caring and compassionate response to others online as well as face-to-face. In doing this, education may help to provide users with the tools they'll need when engaging with technology. After all, technology simply cannot be ignored or avoided without disengaging from society.

References

Alexander, B., & Levine, A. (2008). Web 2.0. Storytelling: Emergence of a new genre. A new wave of innovation for teaching and learning. *Educause Review*, 40–56. Retrieved November 24, 2016, from umwblogs.org

Australian Competition and Consumer Commission. *Scamwatch*. Retrieved from www.scamwatch.gov.au/get-help/real-life-stories.

Chandler, A. (December 15, 2014). The roots of #IllRideWithYou: How Monday's hostage crisis in Sydney spawned a social-media movement against anti-Muslim intolerance. *The Atlantic*. Retrieved April 4, 2017, from www.theatlantic.com/international/archive/2014/12/illridewithyou-hashtag-sydney-siege-anti-islam-australia/383765/

Clark, A., & Chalmers, D. (1998). The extended mind. *Analysis, 58*(1), 7–19.

Cope, B., & Kalantzis, M. (Eds.). (2000). *Multiliteracies: Literacy learning and the design of social futures*. London: Routledge.

D'Olimpio, L. (2015). Trust, well-being and the community of philosophical inquiry. *He Kupu, 4*(2) Special Issue 'Well-being in Early Childhood Education', 45–57.

D'Olimpio, L. (2016). Trust as a virtue in education. *Educational Philosophy and Theory*, Special Issue 'Trust and Schooling' Ed. Bruce Haynes. DOI: 10.1080/00131857.2016.1194737 http://dx.doi.org/10.1080/00131857.2016.1194737

Edwards, R., & Usher, R. (2008). *Globalisation and pedagogy: Space, place, and identity* (2nd ed.). London: Routledge.

Forgas, J. P. (2007). Why sad is better than happy: Mood effects on the persuasiveness of persuasive messages. *Journal of Experimental Social Psychology, 43*, 513–528.

Forgas, J. P. (2017, March 31). Why are some people more gullible than others? *The Conversation*. Retrieved April 4, 2017, from https://theconversation.com/why-are-some-people-more-gullible-than-others-72412

Forgas, J. P., & East, R. (2008). On being happy and gullible: Mood effects on scepticism and the detection of deception. *Journal of Experimental Social Psychology, 44*, 1362–1367.

Gee, J. P. (2009). Reflections on reading Cope and Kalantzis' " 'Multiliteracies': New Literacies, New Learning". *Pedagogies: An International Journal, 4*(3): 196–204.

Hoax-Slayer website: www.hoax-slayer.com/

Kahneman, D. (2011). *Thinking fast and slow*. New York: Farrar, Straus and Giroux.

Marwick, A. E. (2013). *Status update: Celebrity, publicity, and branding in the social media age*. New Haven: Yale University Press.

McAfee, N. (2015). Acting politically in a digital age. In D. Allen & J. S. Light (Eds.), *From voice to influence: Understanding citizenship in a digital age* (pp. 273–292). Chicago: University of Chicago Press.

McLuhan, M. (1964/1995). *Understanding media*. Cambridge: MIT Press.

The online Cambridge Dictionary, Cambridge University Press, 2017. Retrieved January 16, 2017, from http://dictionary.cambridge.org/dictionary/english

Preece, P. F. W., & Baxter, J. H. (2000). Scepticism and gullibility: The superstitious and pseudo-scientific beliefs of secondary school students. *International Journal of Science Education, 22*(11), 1147–1156. http://dx.doi.org/10.1080/095006900 50166724 04/04/2017

Schulman, Y. (2010). *Catfish*. DVD. Dir. H. Joost & A. Schulman. New York City: Supermache.

Snopes.com website: www.snopes.com/

Zelnio, K. (March 14, 2012). On Slacktivism: Lessons from #Kony2012. *Scientific American*. Retrieved April 5, 2017, from https://blogs.scientificamerican.com/evo-eco-lab/on-slacktavism-lessons-from-kony2012/

5 Teaching critical perspectivism

In this chapter, I will focus on the role educational institutions and educators may take to support students to develop a critically perspectival attitude. I am particularly interested in how the study of philosophy, as taught using the philosophy for children (P4C) methodology such as the community of inquiry (CoI), can help young people practice critical thinking skills, collaborative learning techniques and caring dispositions. In order to be able to adopt an attitude of critical perspectivism, one requires the intellectual virtue of discernment, along with other critical thinking skills and moral habits. These skills and attributes will set the learner up as a global citizen who is able to ascertain how best, on balance, to proceed with respect to the information they receive. This will include judging evidence and criteria before deciding what to believe, how they should react or respond to information, images, stories, and others, and in which ways they should (or should not) propagate such information.

Critical perspectivism is an attitude of being critically and compassionately engaged with multiple perspectives. This moral attitude may be modelled, imparted and practised such that those adopting it may engage critically and ethically with, for instance, the technological tools that are ubiquitous in everyday life. To be critically perspectival is to be critically discerning of the information and narratives one is being told, whether these stories are received offline or online, while also being compassionately aware of the fact that others with whom one engages are thinking and feeling human beings much like oneself. Critical perspectivism is important because there will always be various perspectives presented on any given subject, and we have more access to a range of diverse opinions and arguments than ever previously thanks to our smart technology. Importantly, this pluralism does not result in a denial of shared values as, despite personal, cultural and social variance, there is still a shared common humanity. It is this common humanity and a recognition that others are vulnerable to suffering that allows for compassion to be felt as a rational emotion that may guide moral decision making and ethical responses in relation to the information we receive and stories or images we see and hear. By balancing compassionate responses with critical assessment as appropriate to the situation at hand, critical perspectivism is an attitude that assists moral agents to best decide what they should believe, and what they should do.

If it is claimed that the study of philosophy assists those who study it to be better able to adopt the attitude of critical perspectivism, it must be demonstrated that the study of philosophy encourages and supports students to be critical as well as compassionate. It must also teach students how to judge various claims and consider diverse points of view, weighing different perspectives and arguments against one another in order to reach a decision. Such a decision may be about what to believe or what to do. I shall begin by considering how the study of philosophy trains critical thinking skills and then I shall focus on how the community of inquiry pedagogy facilitates and supports critical, caring and collaborative responses to others. In this way I am defending the claim that philosophy can, when done in a particular way, be used by educators to offer students a space to practise and habituate critical perspectivism. This is not to say that every student of philosophy who participates in CoIs *will* become critically perspectival as a result. Furthermore, this is not to deny that one may learn to be critically perspectival elsewhere – in life, in school, at home, or perhaps it comes quite naturally to some. However, it certainly takes effort and is not easy to be both critically and compassionately engaged in the world. Most of the time, we tend to react instinctively according to habit, emotional, or psychological responses we have in relation to the world. As such, anything that can teach and further encourage individuals to adopt the attitude of critical perspectivism is a good thing, and I claim that teaching philosophy to students from a young age, incorporating the CoI methodology, is ideally suited to doing so.

√ Critical thinkers

The study of philosophy is best suited to teaching critical thinking skills that are useful in all areas of study, and life. This is not to say that critical thinking skills aren't taught elsewhere, or learned through experience in the world, because of course they are. However, it is the case that the discipline of philosophy is specifically and explicitly focussed on the teaching, learning and practice of critical thinking. The tools that enable critical thinkers to be reasonable and logical include the skills involved in making and defending arguments as well as critically analysing the ideas and arguments made by others. Such skills include conceptual analysis, deductive and inductive reasoning, sound argumentation, logical inference, consistent thinking, critical analysis, convincing reason giving, the consideration of assumptions and premises, as well as the ability to identify fallacies and flaws in claims and arguments made and defended. These are the skills and techniques that philosophers specifically employ, and when teaching philosophy to students, these are the skills that are assessed and tested as a sign of the students' progress and achievement in the subject.

In defending the idea that the study of philosophy gives rise to critical thinkers, we need to firstly consider the intellectual and cognitive tools a critical thinker possesses. Harvey Siegel (1980) explicitly defends critical thinking as an educational ideal and claims that many educational theorists defend or implicitly assume that critical thinking is a necessary outcome of education. He sums up critical thinking as "as an embodiment of the ideal of rationality" (Siegel, 1980, p. 8) which links the understanding of reasonable arguments to the reasons given in defence of such claims. In this way, critical thinking is principled, and, as such, non-arbitrary. Critical thinkers, then, seek evidence to substantiate claims and assess claims in light of this evidence. Siegel (1988, p. 23) defines the critical thinker in the following manner: "A critical thinker, then, is one who is appropriately moved by reasons: she has the propensity or disposition to believe and act in accordance with reasons; and she has the ability to properly assess the force of reasons in the many contexts in which reasons play a role". In this way, philosophy can be seen to provide students with a good training ground in critical thinking, given that the tools honed by philosophers aim distinctly at providing sound reasoning in defence of one's arguments and assessing claims in light of the reasons provided as evidence for their validity. In fact, Siegel states that the extent to which a pedagogy does encourage critical thinking is a good way by which we can judge the success of the educational program (Siegel, 1980, p. 20).

As the study of philosophy is uniquely suited to teach children general thinking skills that are necessary to academic and practical pursuits, a strong case may be made for its inclusion in the school curriculum. Carrie Winstanley (2008) defends the inclusion of philosophy in the school curriculum in the United Kingdom on the grounds that it has the capacity to develop children's thinking, particularly in light of the inclusion of 'thinking skills' in the U.K. national curriculum. Winstanley argues that it is the study of philosophy that will best equip students with the tools they require to be effective thinkers. She claims:

> Philosophy is the best possible subject for helping children to become effective critical thinkers. It is the subject that can teach them better than any other how to assess reasons, defend positions, define terms, evaluate sources of information, and judge the value of arguments and evidence.
>
> (Winstanley, 2008, p. 95)

The argument can also be made in Australia, given that two of the seven general capabilities listed in the National Australian Curriculum are critical and creative thinking, and ethical understanding. Furthermore, the idea of philosophy as generally educationally beneficial is not at all new. From Socrates wandering the streets of Ancient Greece, speaking with the Athenians, to Bertrand Russell in his 1946 essay *Philosophy for Laymen*, there are philosophers throughout the Western tradition who have defended the view that philosophy should be a part of general education.

Philosophy in schools

Philosophy in schools, or philosophy for and/or with children (P4C), is a movement that started in the United States of America in the 1970s. Matthew Lipman, from Montclair State University, along with Ann Margaret Sharp, started P4C in order to encourage children to think for themselves with a view to becoming reasonable and democratic citizens. Drawing upon the pragmatism of John Dewey (1997; 2004) and the developmental psychology of Lev Vygotsky, Lipman (1988; 2003) believed that philosophy need not be confined to the domain of the academy, but, rather, children from the age of three years old and upwards (primary and senior school–aged students) were capable of critical thinking. Lipman believed that critical and creative thinking require one another, that, to be critical, one requires creativity to think through complex problems and, in order to effectively use these transferable thinking skills, one must practice using them. Based on this combination, the pedagogical tool of the community of inquiry (CoI) became central to his theory. The CoI sees students learning to be critical, creative and caring in a collaborative learning space. Lipman, along with Sharp and Laurance J. Splitter, recognised the affective component of democratic, reasonable citizens and thus highlighted the importance of teaching children to be caring and to work together collaboratively. Thus, P4C aims at creating critical, creative, caring and collaborative thinkers.

While this approach has its roots in the analytic philosophical tradition of America, P4C has been successfully implemented in many countries including the United Kingdom, Australia, Austria, Brazil, Hong Kong, Ireland, Mexico, Portugal, Spain, Singapore and Taiwan (Pritchard, 2014). Philosophy is taught in primary and high schools across the world to students aged between three (3) and seventeen (17) years of age. The pragmatist origins of P4C have not limited researchers or practitioners to use this theory only in their considerations of how philosophy can and should be taught to school-aged students. It is the case, however, that American pragmatism, espoused by thinkers such as Charles Sanders Peirce, John Dewey and Henry James, supports a holistic approach to education which envisions learning as praxis. In following Hilary Putnam (1995, preface), pragmatism can be taken as a way of thinking, not just a movement that peaked at the end of the nineteenth and the beginning of the twentieth century. What is useful about pragmatism taken in this sense, and indeed endorsed by Peirce, James and Dewey, is the commitment to tolerance and pluralism, values which Putnam rightly points out are shared moral beliefs. The radical empirical underpinnings of pragmatism have led its supporters to often speak about truth as the 'fate of thought' or the 'final opinion'; "not that which is presently confirmed, but [that which] is 'fated' to be confirmed, if inquiry is continued long enough, and in a responsible and fallibilistic spirit" (Putnam, 1995, p. 11). And it is this idea that Lipman (2004) picks up from the pragmatists, utilising Peirce's term that was originally applied to a scientific community of inquiry, to explain how philosophical thinking skills should be taught in a classroom environment to encourage critically and yet empathetically engaged dialogue that aims at truth.

Educationalists who support teaching philosophy to school-aged children must also defend the claim that students *can* be taught philosophy. Young people are certainly very good at asking philosophical questions. Gareth Matthews (1980) calls children 'natural philosophers' due to this ability of young children to ponder classical philosophical questions about human nature, knowledge, belief and value that are central to the discipline of Philosophy. Many of the 'why' questions young children ask are reminiscent of great, classical philosophical minds who asked and explored the answers to those very questions. Yet there is more to the study of philosophy and critical thinking than solely the asking of good, philosophical questions (although this is a good place to start).

Michael Hand (2008, p. 5, original italics) points out that it is "*answering questions of a particular kind by means of appropriate methods of investigation*" that is of particular relevance to whether the ensuing discussion is philosophical. This will involve making epistemic progress in a discussion as the dialogue moves towards better answers, towards truth, and away from worse answers. Further skills involved in the study of philosophy include conceptual analysis and the evaluation of arguments, the same skills required by critical thinkers. Philosophy can be taught to young students and they are capable of learning these skills. There must be a consideration of age-appropriate examples, texts and exercises taught in the philosophy classroom, but such considerations do not prevent philosophical understanding and epistemic progress being made in the classroom. Children can, from a young age, understand and analyse the concept of fairness, for instance, and teachers can evaluate the improvement in their students' understanding of such concepts. Improved student understanding may be evident in the contributions made in discussions or written responses given after the students have reflected on the dialogue.

Clinton Golding (2012) defends the importance of epistemic, and thus philosophical, progress being made in the P4C classroom. If we are to evaluate a student's understanding as 'better' *after* the philosophical discussion or CoI dialogue on fairness (for example) has occurred, we are signifying that the student has learnt something of importance or significance relevant to that concept. Golding explains:

- "Better than" describes a relation that exists between two things. In the case of epistemic progress, this epistemic relation holds between two ideas, judgments, or conceptions. Thus epistemic progress describes a two-place predicate – specifically, "x is epistemically better than y" – rather than a one-place predicate such as "x is known" or "x is justified."
- "Better than" also admits of degrees – it is what Philip Cam calls a "scalar" relation – rather than being a discrete category. There is a continuum of epistemic progress because there are degrees of better and worse ideas.

(Golding, 2012, p. 679)

It is due to these features that teachers may assess the cognitive thinking skills exhibited in a philosophical discussion. Reflecting upon the concepts and the students' contributions also allows for participants in the discussion, including the teacher or CoI facilitator, to recognise when epistemic progress has been made. This will be recognisable and may be summed up in the form of comments such as "we have a better understanding of the concept of fairness after that discussion" or "that was a better definition" or "we're getting somewhere in trying to answer the question, but we haven't yet reached a solution". Evaluative comments such as these can be seen as judgements as to whether a claim is justified, or an argument is sound, or a definition is useful and accurate. The defence of such arguments, the justification of claims, and the clarifying of necessary and sufficient conditions when trying to define a concept are all cognitive tools that can be taught. One way philosophical thinking skills can be taught, and philosophical dialogue and progress can be witnessed, is by using the CoI pedagogy as practised by proponents of P4C.

The community of inquiry

The philosophical community of inquiry (CoI) is the pedagogical method practised by P4C practitioners. A teacher will usually commence a lesson with a provocation such as a text (for example, an age-appropriate story, an object, a video, an image or a news headline) and students' questions will be sought through a brainstorming session or in pairs. One exercise to help students express and identify philosophical questions is 'the Question Quadrant' (Cam, 2006). After reading a story, for instance, students may brainstorm questions that emerge from engaging with the text and can then categorise them into one of four spaces on the quadrant designated as 'open' or 'closed' questions (horizontal axis), or 'textual' or 'intellectual' questions (vertical axis). A question is considered philosophical if it is open, 'deep', and does not yield an immediately obvious answer. Philosophical questions will be those placed within the 'open' and 'intellectual' quadrant within Cam's Question Quadrant. These questions differ to questions which can be answered by looking in the text (closed, textual), or by asking an expert (closed, intellectual), or by using one's imagination (open, textual). A philosophical question invites contemplation and wonder and will generate multiple answers, even though some answers will be more reasonable, justified and sound than others. It is philosophical questioning that is at the heart of a well-functioning CoI, along with trust and an empathetic engagement with others.

After reading through a text and playing an activity such as, for instance, a concept game (see Cam, 2016), one can use the Question Quadrant (or another method) to draw out philosophical questions focussed on the central theme the teacher wishes to explore. After collecting the students' philosophical questions, displaying them, and democratically voting on or deciding upon one in order to stimulate dialogue, the classroom is arranged into a CoI. The CoI sees participants seated in an inward-facing circle with the teacher acting as a facilitator of the discussion rather than the authoritative source of all knowledge. This radically alters the traditional role of the teacher whose purpose is not to teach facts which are memorised by students in preparation for testing, but, rather, to encourage students to explore ideas and engage in a dialogue for its own sake, using the chosen question as the focal point of the discussion. The CoI sees participants willing to critically engage with their own and others' ideas, while compassionately responding to the views of others as they are encountered. As Haynes (2014, pp. 1201–1202, citing Lipman, 1988, 1991/2003) explains:

> The community of inquiry has a structure which evokes the spirit of cooperation, care, trust, safety, and a sense of common purpose and inquiry,

which, in turn, evokes a form of self-correcting practice driven by the need to transform that which is intriguing, problematic, confused, ambiguous or fragmentary into some kind of unifying whole which is satisfying to those involved.

This aiming at a sense of satisfaction relates to the desire of participants in a CoI to enjoy a good philosophical dialogue (namely, a dialogue that makes epistemic and philosophical progress) and reach some sort of settlement in relation to the ideas discussed and analysed. The initial philosophical question points to a problem the participants in a CoI are seeking to explore or, ultimately, resolve, and this inquiring disposition (as Splitter, 2016 calls it) indicates a desire to progress from a *state of unsettlement* (or tension) to one of *settlement*. Any sense of settlement, along with the claim that epistemic progress can occur within a CoI immediately moves us away from a relativistic pedagogical model where every answer or argument is as good as any other. Instead of thinking that there are 'no correct answers', the philosophical CoI should see participants move further away from the worst answers or arguments and move towards more reasonable, justified ideas. As Splitter (2011) explains:

> Participating in a CoI allows students, individually and collaboratively, to develop their own ideas and perspectives based on appropriately rigorous modes of thinking and against the background of a thorough understanding and appreciation of those ideas and perspectives that, having stood the test of time, may be represented as society's best view of things to date.
>
> (p. 497)

Thus, a well-functioning CoI can be said to make progress. This progress takes the form of philosophical and epistemic progress as defended by Golding. Lipman has endorsed such a position from the outset, claiming:

> First, I think we need to see that the community of inquiry is not aimless. It is a process that aims at producing a *product* – at some kind of settlement or judgement, however partial and tentative this may be. Second, the process has a sense of direction; it moves where the argument takes it. Third, the process is not merely conversation or discussion; it is dialogical. This means it has a structure . . . inquiry has its procedural rules, which are largely logical in nature.
>
> (Lipman, 2003, pp. 83–84)

The progress we hope to find within a CoI should be that of logical argumentation, and a CoI allows for the fact that such inquiry takes place within a context. Lipman reminds us that "Inquiry takes place in situations – in contextual wholes or fields" (2003, p. 85). One can judge a CoI as exhibiting good inquiry or conforming to a logical set of rules, and the conclusions of the inquirers are such as can start to provide a foundation for knowledge. There are epistemic criteria that can be evaluated when they are revealed within the CoI dialogue. Furthermore, the CoI is aiming at such epistemic goals – at truth and knowledge, such that the inquirers feel a sense of settlement that satisfies (even if provisionally) their puzzlement and wonder. Lipman notes, "Settlements provide us with grounds for assuming, warrants for asserting. They represent *provisional judgements* rather than firm bases for absolute convictions" (2003, p. 93). In this way, the CoI is open to further inquiry, to new information, and allows for self-correction. It has a fallibilistic nature, but this does not mean that there are 'no truths', or that there is only relative truth. Rather, there must be truth if we are able to judge the epistemic and philosophical progress towards this goal.

In order for epistemic progress to be made, the teacher should be trained in both philosophy and the CoI pedagogy. Lipman advocated using purpose-written narratives in the P4C classroom, such as his *Harry Stottlemeier's Discovery* (1974). Narratives are a wonderful stimulus because they are interesting and engaging, and they encourage an imaginative response towards the characters and scenarios therein depicted. P4C novels such as Lipman's are imbued with philosophical themes exploring issues such as friendship, ethics, metaphysics, religious belief, epistemology and aesthetics while being written for an age-appropriate audience. Teachers as facilitators of philosophical dialogue must develop a philosophical ear so as to recognise when particular contributions are philosophical or philosophically promising and encourage the dialogue to focus on and further investigate these themes. In this way, CoI participants will spend more time critically investigating philosophical questions and topics.

In a philosophy class or CoI, teachers should also assist the students to recognise when fallacious reasoning is occurring and invite participants in the dialogue to challenge their own assumptions, as well as those of others. As such, P4C and the CoI build critically reflective thinking skills (Sharp, 2007). Lipman defines critical thinking as "thinking that (1) facilitates judgment because it (2) relies on criteria, (3) is self-correcting, and (4) is sensitive to context" (Lipman, 2003, p. 212). These critical thinking skills are accompanied by "caring" and "creative" thinking as equally important skills that children are encouraged to develop in a CoI as they recognise themselves as members of a community of inquirers, jointly interested in uncovering truth (Lipman, 2003; Splitter & Sharp, 1995).

The CoI also fosters a feeling of trust and care about the well-being of the members of its group. It aims at inclusiveness, even when the arguments and ideas of individual members differ. Generalised trust is imperative for society to function well, as it allows for citizens to recognise one another as more similar rather than dissimilar to ourselves. A sense of fellow-feeling engendered by trust allows us to compassionately respond to others, to trust strangers and recognise that everyone has a set of human rights or capabilities that ought to be protected. These features allow us to feel safe, where appropriate, and this is something for which we should aim within our various communities, including online communities. Generalised trust and care or compassion is sorely needed in a global world, connected by Internet technologies.

For children to practice trusting, alongside critical discernment, and to develop trustworthiness is vital not only at home but also in relation to the school environment. Part of what builds confidence in children is enabling them to trust themselves and their own judgement, and supporting this self-belief by demonstrating how their opinions and beliefs are listened to in a respectful manner. One way children may be heard and have room to self-reflect is through the introduction of philosophy with children into the school curriculum, and the participation in CoIs in the classroom. In this way, the critical thinker will not just know what the right thing to do is, they will also know how to go about accomplishing that action while being sensitive to the context and others involved in the situation. It is this contextual application of knowledge and the transferable thinking skills that leads Sharp to claim that the rituals involved in the practice of P4C in a CoI classroom setting can lead to the cultivation of wisdom (2007, p. 13).

Wisdom may be cultivated if the philosophical spirit is imbued in the attitudes of the teacher as well as the students, and when the materials chosen as provocations are suitably philosophical. The word philosophy literally means the love of wisdom: *philo-sophia*. The big questions often dealt with in philosophy refer to value (what is important to us, how do we live a meaningful life, what is good?) and knowledge (epistemological questions such as what can we know and how can we know it?) and these topics and questions simply do not have one obvious answer. Rather, they require interrogation, thought and time for reflection and dialogue. Such qualities mark them as standing in opposition to the neoliberal agenda in an audit culture in which learning objectives are to be quantifiable and measurable. Such qualities also mark them as being useful for life – not just for testing. In this way, the study of philosophy seeks wisdom, not just facts and figures.

Thus, the cultivation of wisdom in young people can be an aim of education only when education is viewed as a holistic practice and not simply the training of vocational skills. Fortunately, taking weekly philosophy classes also improves students' measurable cognitive skills. Empirical research conducted by Topping and Trickey (2007a; 2007b) has demonstrated that children who study philosophy are more likely to achieve better academic results and that they also have additional social benefits such as better self-esteem and increased empathy for others. There is also said to be less bullying in the schoolyard and fewer behaviour management issues (Millett & Tapper, 2012).

A recent study that involved 1500 children across 48 schools in England funded by the Education Endowment Foundation and independently evaluated by a team from Durham University (2015) found that, on average, children who took part in one hour of P4C per week saw two months of progress in their reading and maths outcomes at the end of the school year compared to those who didn't undertake P4C. For disadvantaged students who were fed a school dinner, their writing ability improved by two months, their math skills by three months and their reading abilities by four months. These gains were achieved with the program being delivered for one hour per week at a total annual cost of £16 (AUD $26 / USD $20) per pupil (Gorard, S., Siddiqui, N., & See, B. H., 2016). These quantifiable outcomes are useful when trying to persuade school boards, parents and governmental curriculum advisors of the use value of teaching philosophy as a discrete subject area. Yet they are also, simply, additional benefits to the fact that good philosophical dialogue is valuable in and of itself. The aim of philosophy for children is to teach students to carefully consider diverse ideas, be self-reflective and empathise with others.

Thus it can be seen that by studying philosophy and participating in a well-functioning CoI, students may learn to be critical thinkers who are inclusive and caring towards one another. The CoI offers teachers a pedagogical method by which students can practice critical, creative, caring and collaborative thinking skills. It has been argued that these thinking skills will encourage students to be reasonable and democratic, to treat others fairly and to be open to reconsidering their own ideas as they seek evidence for beliefs (Burgh, Field & Freakley, 2006). These are the skills required for one to be able to adopt the attitude of critical perspectivism, and these are also contemporary skills that are sorely needed in today's society.

How the CoI can assist in educating multiliteracies

Teaching children philosophy in the classroom using a CoI can help develop important skills that reasonable citizens employ in their daily lives. This notion of habituation and learning by doing can see the skills practised in a CoI then be applied to Media and Web 2.0. P4C is a holistic approach to education that recognises that educators are preparing students for life, as opposed to solely equipping them with a set of vocational skills. The CoI sees philosophy as a praxis and provides young people with a safe space whereby they can speak and be heard, challenging while simultaneously refining their ideas and thought processes. In seeking truth amid diverse voices, the CoI provides a forum in which students are required to critically engage with diverse opinions, examples and arguments in search of justified true belief as well as wisdom (*phronesis*). These are the same skills required when sifting through the information widely accessible on the Internet, information that constantly bombards us as we increasingly use social media platforms as a means by which to gain access to news, gossip, images and information. By encouraging compassionate engagement with others while also critically assessing diverse ideas, the CoI can also train young people to have empathetic habits, with the hope that such caring dispositions become habitual responses to others. In this way, one may respond to others compassionately, whether those others are encountered face-to-face or are avatars encountered in an online environment, including competitive online environments such as augmented reality gameworlds. Furthermore, by incorporating mass media and social media examples into the CoI pedagogy in the P4C classroom, children are given the opportunity to learn multiliteracy competencies which they are then able to apply online.

One example of an activity that can be done in a P4C classroom, leading to a CoI on the subject of gender, utilises images of people, including celebrities, found on the Internet as a stimulus. Given that much of the online content we receive, create and share is pictorial (selfies, memes, images and photos assail our vision as soon as we log on to any new media technology), this activity can offer a good opportunity to encourage a dialogue about self-representation and gender-defined norms (nature vs nurture) within a safe environment in the classroom. Obviously, the pictures should be chosen and the discussion facilitated at an age-appropriate level by a teacher who is familiar with their students. Images chosen could be used to explore the way celebrities portray themselves and whether there are certain socially constructed gender pressures to represent oneself in a particular manner, thereby creating a space for dialogue and for students to critique these 'ideals'. Truisms such as 'don't judge a book by its cover' and 'do unto others as you'd have them do to you' could also be considered and discussed. The dialogue would hopefully stimulate critical and empathetic thinking in its participants and encourage them to reflect on how they portray themselves online, and how they might wish to be viewed.

By educating students to be critical, the study of philosophy can be used to refine and habituate cognitive skills that are sorely needed in today's technological society. The empirical evidence that correlates improved cognitive thinking skills with weekly philosophy classes has been detailed above in the studies done by Topping and Trickey and the Education Endowment Foundation.[1] Philosophical thinking skills ensure that critical thinkers are good at problem solving, creative in their approach to seeking solutions to dilemmas, critically able to assess arguments in terms of justifiable reasons and unchecked assumptions, sound premises and conclusions that logically follow. However, such critical thinking skills that enable a student to score well on literacy and numeracy tests are alone insufficient to help them navigate the complex ethical dilemmas we experience in life. It is the CoI praxis that provides participants with richly contextual dialogue and encounters that challenge our preconceived notions. The CoI dialogue also encourages compassion as a rational emotion and such moral virtue is underpinned by the recognition that fellow participants in a dialogue are embodied, thinking and feeling human beings much like oneself. As Sprod (2001, p. 183) notes, these virtues, such as trust and respect, may be cultivated within a CoI and then may extend beyond the CoI:

> Although students may or may not join willingly, for it to work, the community must soon build communalities. Chief will be the interest in the inquiry itself, allied to a growing trust in the community's members as fellow inquirers. Part of that reliance on others will arise from the recognition and valuing of diversity within the community: diversity of views, of learning approaches, of styles of reasonableness. And finally, there may well come a recognition that the boundaries of the classroom community of inquiry are porous; that this community does not exclude outsiders, and that the capacities learned in the community apply outside it.

Communicating with others in this holistic manner, employing critical discernment along with empathy, should also be applied to online information, media sites and social media participation. This sums up the attitude I call critical perspectivism, which is an appropriate way to engage ethically with others, face-to-face or in an online mediated forum. It is an attitude that can be taught and then practised, and P4C and the CoI is one way in which this can be done. Critical perspectivism is always useful, and pragmatic, yet it is particularly important in contemporary society given that technological devices and tools are designed in such a way as to encourage immediate and instinctive engagement with others as well as with ideas. One who adopts a critically perspectival attitude will necessarily slow down and consider *how* and *why* they are using social media; this moral agent will reflect upon how they may best glean information from online (and other) sources, and they will be disposed to check before they further share, like or otherwise spread the image or text if propagating such a message is a *good* or virtuous thing to do.

Of course, here I am assuming that if participants in a CoI learn to be critically perspectival, they will, eventually, conduct themselves in this manner outside of the CoI, or classroom, or school environment. To the contrary, we can imagine situations in which students are constructively critical and compassionate towards one another within a CoI, but then do not behave in this way in the school playground, at home, or online. Ultimately it will be up to each individual to choose how they wish to conduct themselves and what kind of person they want to be. This is a puzzle moral philosophers know only too well: being aware of and familiar with moral guidelines or rules is insufficient when it comes to moral or virtuous character. However, as educationalists will espouse, we cannot underestimate the role of education and role models (in many different forms) for providing a good example towards others. One of the reasons I am emphasising the need for individuals to learn how to be critically perspectival in relation to Web 2.0 is precisely because of the lack of educational spaces and role models that openly discuss how to engage with information received from online sources and social media platforms in a critical as well as ethically engaged manner. Students are learning more from their peers and by trial and error than from teachers and parents because, particularly at this time of transition, the students are the digital natives where as their usual role models are still learning the language of multiliteracies.

In an effort to emphasize the positive links between learning how to be critically perspectival and how to apply critical perspectivism to Web 2.0, educators (and parents) need to open up a constructive dialogue about multiliteracies. One way to do this is by addressing the subject matter deliberately in P4C classes and consciously including relevant examples in exercises and activities. The philosophical questions generated about Web 2.0 and smart technology may then be used as the focal theme for ensuing CoIs. Facilitators of such CoIs will undoubtedly learn just as much from these dialogues as the participants. One example of an activity that can be conducted within a P4C class involves gathering a variety of reports on a specific event or issue that have been shared online via various sources. The diverse reports may range from credible news websites to other journalistic reporting of various standards (i.e. these could be local, national or international), blog posts, wiki entries and Buzzfeed listicles as well as Tweets or Facebook posts all on the topic. With these as the provocation materials, concept games could be played around how true they are (to interrogate accuracy of reporting and how it can be judged that one version of events is more or less factual than another), how objective or emotive the reports are, or how they made the viewer feel. The texts may be categorised onto continuums ranging from TRUE → FALSE; or OBJECTIVE → SUBJECTIVE; or even EMPOW-ERING → DISEMPOWERING; or three circles could be used, such as "Accu-rate", "Inaccurate", and "?". The activities may be done individually, in pairs, or small groups prior to generating student questions (possibly using a Question Quadrant), after which one philosophical question may be selected from which to facilitate a CoI dialogue.

Due to the nature of the CoI dialogue that takes as its focus the students' own questions, and allows for students' contributions to actively shape the dialogue as it unfolds, there is a high level of interest in the discussion by the participants. There is a tangible feeling of connection and excitement when one is a part of a well-functioning CoI. When a CoI is harmonious and energised, even the teacher as facilitator feels a part of a community of inquirers investigating ideas and test-ing out examples. These ideas and examples are important and they matter, as they often pertain to how we live our lives and make meaning. After all, philo-sophical themes and topics may also link to real life and are often versions of the perennial questions upon which reflective thinkers pontificate. Such perennial questions may take on a contemporary garb and ask about truth *online*, or they may ask about online communication or friendships – yet these are simply exten-sions of classical philosophical questions such as 'What is the good life?'

It must be noted that the well-functioning CoI does not occur automatically, and some prerequisites are required. These include some level of initial trust amongst members of the group, and a well-trained facilitator. The role of the facilitator is crucial and Gardner (2015) points out that facilitating is hard work! The facilitator of a CoI has to develop a philosophical ear while pushing for depth and truth. Gardener (2015, p. 82) suggests that we think about this push as asking for the '*second* why'. It is this going 'deeper' that often characterises dialogue that is *philosophical* as opposed to simply good conversation. The cru-cial role of the facilitator within the CoI highlights the importance of teacher training. Again drawing upon the Deweyian notion of learning-by-doing, the teachers themselves should take the time to participate in CoIs amongst peers, so that they have the experience of what it feels like to be within a CoI. Kennedy (2015) points out that useful topics for teachers to discuss within a CoI include their own philosophy of childhood which gives them a chance to explore their assumptions and experiences about what children are like. Kennedy believes that by encouraging teachers to have this discussion, they are better able to be aware of, and possibly set aside some of their pre-conceived notions that limit the wis-dom associated with what children know. By setting aside preconceptions about childhood, teachers are then able to better listen and respond to children's voices and ideas. This experience of participating in a CoI with peers is thus of benefit to those who then facilitate CoIs; it is a worthwhile practice in and of itself, but also serves as professional development and assist facilitators to train their philo-sophical ear.

The collaborative CoI setting is one place in which participants can learn to be critically reflective while also attending empathetically to others. It is by encouraging such cognitive and affective skills that the CoI offers participants the opportunity to practice critical perspectivism. In the ways described above, the CoI asks participants to practice the virtues while also reflecting upon them (Sprod, 2001, p. 162) because it "formalizes and makes more explicit the communicative action and discourse in which children will have frequently engaged" (Sprod, 2001, p. 159). This formalising aspect of dialogue within the CoI creates space for participants to reflect upon their ideas as well as the ideas of others, which includes how these ideas are conveyed and received within a social setting. Such education encourages students to think for themselves, which is precisely what Lipman and advocates of P4C wish to encourage. If this is indeed what the CoI teaches people to do, then they will be able to do so online as well as face-to-face.

Conclusion

Educators and educational institutions have an important role to play both in traditional classroom and other face-to-face spaces, as well as online. Creating spaces for intelligent dialogue and the respectful exchange of ideas is vital if we wish to cultivate a society of reflective and compassionate individuals who support autonomy and diversity while recognising a common humanity. The skills involved in critical perspectivism are those cognitive and affective skills that support such a society. The individual who adopts an attitude of critical perspectivism is a person who cares about the truth and about other people and is deeply engaged with ideas and moral questions. It has been argued that there are some things we must learn by doing as we aim at practical wisdom, and we cannot escape the fact that we are embodied, rational, as well as affective beings. This means that we must look at ideas and decisions contextually, and try to adopt as many diverse perspectives as possible in an effort to get closer to the truth. One way by which we can achieve this is to recognise that we coexist with others who may have different points of view to our own. By entering into a dialogue, we can learn to see from another's perspective, even while always recognising that we are also necessarily limited by our own subjective point of view. Dialogue is a crucial skill that is learned and refined through practice and the benefit of the CoI method as practised by P4C practitioners is that it explicitly attends to the skills of dialogue, including argumentation and the logical progression from premises through to justified conclusions. Additionally, this is done in a safe educational space that prioritises hearing various stories – including and particularly attending to children's voices. The CoI does not discount the wisdom any single individual has to offer, even while honouring the idea that our collective wisdom is greater than the sum of its parts.

Humans are great innovators, able to be creative and flexible in our pedagogical practices. The role for educators to help children (and adults) learn the skills of critical thinking, caring dispositions, and how to work together collaboratively is valid for as long as humans cohabit. If such skills can be developed alongside or in conjunction with multiliteracies, these people will have the best chance of becoming critical, caring, and reasonable citizens who engage ethically with others both face-to-face and online. The study of philosophy and the pedagogical tool of the CoI is one way such holistic education can occur in a classroom setting. Teachers of philosophy for children aim at producing reasonable, democratic citizens whose transferable cognitive thinking tools will provide them with a good set of vocational and life skills, supported by moral intentions and appropriate affective dispositions.

These skills are necessary because we live in a global society and are more connected than ever previously, impacting upon one another as we live, work and make use of the earth's resources. As always in a neoliberal technological society, there are multiple ways of teaching such skills, yet I defend the centrality of dialogue as an eternal pedagogical praxis. As such, I have offered P4C and the CoI as a way to educate students in such a way that they are able to adopt the attitude of critical perspectivism where required, both online and elsewhere. I look forward to being surprised in future years by new ways in which educational spaces will be reimagined.

Note

1 The Education Endowment Foundation of the UK has just awarded SAPERE (The Society for the Advancement of Philosophical Enquiry and Reflection in Education) a £1,204,000 grant to further test the empirical results of children studying philosophy on children's social skills and cognitive abilities. The results of this second study will be published in 2021. See https://educationendowmentfoundation.org.uk/our-work/projects/sapere-philosophy-for-children-effectiveness-trial/ for more details.

References

Burgh, G., Field, T., & Freakley, M. (2006). *Ethics and the community of inquiry: Education for deliberative democracy.* Melbourne, Australia: Thomson.

Cam, P. (2006). *Twenty thinking tools.* Camberwell, Victoria, Australia: ACER. A modified version of the Question Quadrant retrieved from www.philosophyineducation.com/resources/Question+Quadrant.pdf

Cam, P. (2016). Basic operations in reasoning and conceptual analysis. *Journal of Philosophy in Schools, 3*(2), 7–18. Retrieved from www.ojs.unisa.edu.au/index.php/jps/article/view/1347/875

Dewey, J. (1997). *How we think.* Mineola, NY: Dover Publications. (Original work published 1910).

Dewey, J. (2004). *Democracy and education.* Mineola, NY: Dover Publications. (Original work published 1916).

Education Endowment Foundation. (2015, July). *Philosophy for children: Evaluation report and executive summary.* Independent evaluators: Stephen Gorard, Nadia Siddiqui and Beng Huat See.

Gardner, S. T. (2015). Inquiry is no mere conversation (or discussion or dialogue). Facilitation of inquiry is hard work! *Journal of Philosophy in Schools, 2*(1), 71–91. Retrieved from www.ojs.unisa.edu.au/index.php/jps/article/view/1105/777

Golding, C. (2012). Epistemic progress: A construct for understanding and evaluating inquiry. *Educational Theory, 62*(6), 677–693.

Gorard, S., Siddiqui, N., & See, B. H. (2016). Can 'Philosophy for Children' improve primary school attainment? *Journal of Philosophy of Education* DOI: 10.1111/

1467-9752.12227. Retrieved January 3, 2017, from http://onlinelibrary.wiley.com/doi/10.1111/1467-9752.12227/epdf

Hand, M. (2008). Can children be taught philosophy? In M. Hand & C. Winstanley (Eds.), *Philosophy in schools* (pp. 3–17). London: Continuum.

Haynes, F. (2014). Editorial. *Educational Philosophy and Theory, 46*(11), 1197–1202.

Kennedy, D. (2015). Practicing philosophy of childhood: Teaching in the (r)evolutionary mode. *Journal of Philosophy in Schools, 2*(1), 4–17. Retrieved from www.ojs.unisa.edu.au/index.php/jps/article/view/1099/772

Lipman, M. (1974). *Harry Stottlemeier's discovery*. New York: Columbia University Press.

Lipman, M. (1988). *Philosophy goes to school*. Philadelphia, PA: Temple University Press.

Lipman, M. (2003). *Thinking in education* (2nd ed.). Cambridge: Cambridge University Press.

Lipman, M. (2004). Philosophy for children's debt to Dewey. *Critical and Creative Thinking, 12*(1), 1–8.

Matthews, G. (1980). *Philosophy and the young child*. Cambridge: Harvard University Press.

Millett, S., & Tapper, A. (2012). Benefits of collaborative philosophical inquiry in schools. *Educational Philosophy and Theory, 44*(5), 546–567.

Pritchard, M. (2014). Philosophy for children. In E. N. Zalta (Ed.), *The Stanford encyclopedia of philosophy*. Retrieved August 11, 2016, from http://plato.stanford.edu/archives/spr2014/entries/children/

Putnam, H. (1995). *Pragmatism*. Oxford: Blackwell.

Russell, B. (1946). Philosophy for Laymen. *Universities Quarterly, 1*, 38–49. Reproduced in *Unpopular Essays*, Chapter 2 (George Allen & Unwin, 1951).

Sharp, A. M. (2007). The classroom community of inquiry as ritual: How we can cultivate wisdom. *Critical and Creative Thinking, 15*(1), 3–14.

Siegel, H. (1980). Critical thinking as an educational ideal. *The Educational Forum, 45*(1), 7–23. DOI: 10.1080/00131728009336046

Siegel, H. (1988). *Educating reason: Rationality, critical thinking, and education*. London: Routledge.

Splitter, L. (2011). Identity, citizenship and moral education. *Educational Philosophy and Theory, 43*(5), 484–505.

Splitter, L. (2016). The dispositional ingredients at the heart of questioning and inquiry. *Journal of Philosophy in Schools, 3*(2), 18–39. Retrieved from www.ojs.unisa.edu.au/index.php/jps/article/view/1348/876

Splitter, L., & Sharp, A. M. (1995). *Teaching for better thinking: The classroom community of inquiry*. Melbourne, Australia: ACER.

Sprod, T. (2001). *Philosophical discussion in moral education: The community of ethical inquiry*. London: Routledge.

Topping K. J., & Trickey, S. (2007a). Collaborative philosophical enquiry for school children: Cognitive gains at two-year follow-up. *British Journal of Educational Psychology, 77*(4), 787–796.

Topping, K. J., & Trickey, S. (2007b). Impact of philosophical enquiry on school students' interactive behaviour. *Thinking Skills and Creativity, 2*(2), 73–84.

Winstanley, C. (2008). Philosophy and the development of critical thinking. In M. Hand & C. Winstanley (Eds.), *Philosophy in schools* (pp. 85–95). London: Continuum.

6 Philosophy in the public sphere

For many people, the online world of Web 2.0 is carried around with us wherever we go, thanks to smart technology, and is a very real part of our lives. Mobile devices ensure we are connected to others and 'plugged in' to an eternal stream of information and images 24/7. At a time in which we have more access to facts, opinions, images, stories, games and people than ever previously, it is imperative that we aim to make our interaction with and contribution to this global village as informed, ethical and respectful as possible. In the last chapter, I argued that there is an important role for philosophy to play in teaching people how to adopt an attitude of critical perspectivism. This ethical attitude may be applied to information we receive and be used to help us to negotiate the online world in such a way so as to protect us while also enabling us to benefit from its interconnectedness and endless content. I have considered the way philosophy may be taught within schools, classrooms and educational spaces in order to achieve this goal and defended the use of CoIs as a way of facilitating critical perspectivism. In this chapter, I will consider the role of the philosopher and for philosophy outside of the academy and beyond the confines of the classroom. I will consider whether philosophy can and should be done with members of the general public and how this might best occur.

In the opening sentences to *The Offensive Internet: Speech, Privacy and Reputation* (2010, p. 1), Saul Levmore and Martha Nussbaum remark that

> In many ways the Internet has succeeded in remaking us as inhabitants of a small village. No one is a stranger either in the village or on the Internet; in both settings the savvy citizen knows how to process information. The Internet may be offensive to some, as the title of this book warns, but it benefits far more than it offends the well-informed.

It is telling that it is the well-informed and 'savvy' citizen who is more protected and will benefit the most from the ease of access to the collective knowledge (along with everything else) that the Internet has to offer. If this is the case, the important question arises as to how we can educate people to be well-informed and savvy? I have defended the CoI pedagogy practiced by proponents of P4C as a useful method by which to develop and encourage critical, caring, creative and collaborative thinking skills that can be applied to engagement with everyday moral dilemmas, mass art and social media. In other words, participants in CoIs may practice the attitude of critical perspectivism, which may then be applied online or face-to-face when engaging with the stories, information and images that are encountered. Yet there is no reason why CoIs cannot be facilitated outside of educational spaces, with members of the general public, with the potential of encouraging critically perspectival attitudes in those participants.

Public philosophy

In order to be engaged in a critically perspectival manner, one must be educated to be critical, compassionate and collaborative in one's approach to receiving, understanding and transmitting information. In chapter five, I argued that the study and practise of philosophy in schools allows students to learn how to think critically and to assess arguments for soundness, validity and logical progression while interrogating any assumptions underlying given premises or conclusions. Furthermore, in philosophical communities of inquiry, these critical thinking skills are combined with a care for one's fellow critical thinkers who are also seeking truth, knowledge, and wisdom. By working together in a CoI to collectively make meaning and question ideas, participants are, when all is going well, actively practising critical perspectivism.

Admittedly, the transference of interpersonal, cognitive and affective skills to the online world of Web 2.0 does not fully account for the ways in which such participatory media shapes and disrupts our previously familiar modes of communication and interaction, let alone the ways in which we receive and transmit information, ideas and images. The ways in which such saturated social media spaces affect us also require careful consideration and analysis. Yet, unlike Adorno's worry about mass-produced and distributed cultural products, and also unlike Benjamin's optimism about their ease of accessibility, I shift my focus from the media to the attitude people may adopt in relation to all that is on offer in this technologically infused marketplace of ideas and entertainment. Whatever role philosophers and the study of philosophy can play in assisting people to adopt an attitude of critical perspectivism ought to be embraced and practised with people of all ages. Critical perspectivism is necessary in today's world, because it gives us the ability to engage with multiple perspectives and still judge: to be critical, caring and compassionate while recognising the context in which dialogue and interactions take place.

Given that the well-functioning CoI can foster and cultivate critical perspectivism, there is no reason to think that this cannot be achieved outside of school or classroom environments. It is not only school-aged children who would benefit from practising critical, creative, and caring responses towards others and ideas while engaged in a focussed, collaborative dialogue. The CoI may be used as a tool to facilitate public philosophy events such as philosophy cafés. Philosophy cafés have been around for many years, in many forms, in many diverse countries. Some are run by professional philosophers or those formally educated in the field of philosophy, and others are less formal, simply conducted by enthusiastic individuals. The same criteria will apply to philosophy cafés as they would to a P4C classroom environment if they are to stimulate critical perspectivism. Thus, much will rest on the group dynamic and the skills of the group facilitator. For a philosophy café to function well as a CoI, the facilitator of such an event will have the required skills to be able to keep the dialogue on topic, ensure contributions are made in a respectful manner, and they will also have the requisite philosophical ear to hear when points are being made that delve deeper into the heart of the concept under discussion. It is these philosophical contributions that should be sought, and then pursued in order for the discussion to proceed from interesting conversation to philosophical dialogue.

No doubt, philosophical inquiry can be done *badly*, that is to say, superficially or disrespectfully or uncritically within a classroom space or a public setting such as a philosophy café. In order for a CoI to be philosophical *and* caring, there is an onus on each participant to behave in a certain manner, as well as the required skills of a facilitator. It helps to have a set of rules by which any such group of inquirers agrees to abide. These will include guidelines such as addressing the topic rather than another person so as to avoid the *ad hominem* personal attack, taking turns to speak, do not interrupt others, stay on topic and keep examples relevant, be willing to change your mind in light of new evidence, be prepared to think, and expect multiple ideas to be presented, critiqued and discussed; it is extremely unlikely that everyone will agree. Such guidelines play an important role in establishing a space for dialogue that is respectful and safe for all participants.

If run well, philosophy cafés have the potential to teach members of the wider community how to engage critically and compassionately with philosophical ideas and contemporary issues. Philosophy needn't be confined to the academy, and there are important democratic arguments to be made for conducting philosophical events within public spaces outside of the learned halls of academia. (Similarly, there are good arguments to be made in favour of publishing in open access and other accessible online journals and magazines). In relation to rethinking how philosophy can be done, and in light of social justice concerns, Greene and Griffiths (2008) explore the various ways one can do philosophy and be philosophically engaged in an educational space. Applying a feminist gaze, they tell their personal narratives that led them to where they are now and how they experienced philosophy of education within the academy and associated societies. Acknowledging the lack of employed female academic philosophers, it is important to find ways of allowing various voices to be heard in the discipline of philosophy and philosophy of education, and also of encouraging access to the works of philosophers, and philosophical ideas beyond the limited scope of the academy. Amongst the many options that may meet such criteria, teaching philosophy in schools is an important and viable option, and philosophy cafés is another suitable prospect. Both of these options invite 'the masses' to democratically engage in philosophical dialogue and to cultivate critical perspectivism.

Greene and Griffiths (2008, p. 90) certainly invoke the Adornian spirit, suggesting that children and adults release their imagination to open up spaces in which they can participate in public discourse that allows for a "dialectic of freedom". The image created here is one of radicalising public spaces to allow for autonomous contributions and the unfettered interchange of ideas, a space in which such ideas are interrogated for validity, reasonableness and pragmatic tenacity. This ideal of radical liberation and the associated democratic opening up of dialogue has underscored much of the enthusiasm surrounding the philosophy for children movement and philosophy in schools' literature.

Randell (2004) gives an example of the Fremantle philosophy café in Western Australia as a successful instantiation of an informal community development programme that allows for the manifestation of such liberal ideals. Granted, this particular philosophy café is not run according the P4C/CoI principles, yet the example serves to highlight the importance of participation within public spaces. According to Randell, participation, "defined as a dynamic activity occurring in a 'space'", provides the conditions for creativity and engenders a sense of community and belonging for those who attend and participate. In this way, philosophy cafés have the potential to provide a space for community participation that may serve the well-being of its members and locale, but they also have the possibility of further cultivating the cognitive thinking skills and caring responses of its members. The latter, the cultivation of critical perspectivism, may be achieved if the philosophy café is run in such a way so as to encourage and support the development of critical thinking alongside caring and creative responses by participants to one another as well as to the ideas therein discussed. Philosophy cafés are thus one way in which philosophy may be practised in spaces beyond the academy with members of the general public.

Philosophers as public intellectuals

Another role philosophers may take within the public sphere is associated with the notion of the public intellectual. The public intellectual is an expert within their field who is often sought out to provide commentary on current affairs or explain concepts to a general audience using a variety of media. The public intellectual may write for a newspaper or an online publication such as The Conversation.edu; they might have their own blog or website and publish books for a general readership (whether or not they also publish academic texts). These experts may also be called upon for interviews, to serve as consultants, and may have some influence in the political arena.

If an academic such as a philosopher takes on the role of public intellectual, they may be able to offer an example of what critical perspectivism *looks like in practice*. This may not be the same thing as giving the members of the general public the opportunity to practice critical perspectivism themselves, but it may serve to provide examples of critical and compassionate responses to particular scenarios. Granted, for this to work, the public intellectual in question would indeed themselves have to be appropriately critical as well as compassionate when providing commentary or articulating their arguments, which may not always occur. But to the extent that it does, examples of philosophical dialogue, respectful disagreement and the critical analysis of issues along with compassion displayed towards others who may be vulnerable to suffering offer a model for how this moral attitude may guide what we think, what we say and how we act.

Writing for the *New Statesman*, David Herman laments the contemporary lack of philosophers as recognised sources of wisdom to which politicians and others have access. In particular reference to Britain, Herman proclaims the 1950s to the 1990s as "a golden age of British academic philosophy in mainstream culture". Citing philosophers such as A. J. Ayer, Bernard Williams, Mary Warnock and Noam Chomsky, Herman reminisces about when politicians knew about the work of philosophers living, writing and working at the same time as them. The nature of academic philosophy is increasingly such that there is a great deal of pressure upon academics to publish in reputable journals or with academic publishers so as to meet the neoliberal demands of a 'publish or perish' academic culture. As such, philosophers often end up 'writing for one another' in an attempt to gain employment, strive for tenure or promotion or even, simply, to retain their position within a university that is constantly reconsidering whether or not to renew existing employment contracts. In light of these changes to academia, the dissemination of the work of contemporary philosophers has diminished and narrowed. It is rare that members of the general public and people who do not work in universities (where there is institutional access to such works) can afford to purchase the textbooks or subscribe to the journals in which many academics publish, and even if they do access these works, the texts are often written in a jargon-infused language specific to one's discipline. However, the emergence of smart technology and Web 2.0 is again altering the current landscape of ideas.

With access to Web 2.0, including social media platforms, philosophers and other academics are increasingly able to speak directly to the public. On Twitter, for instance, @TrueSciPhi analyses the number of Philosophers on Twitter, including Philosophy Organisations and podcasts, all of which are ranked in a couple of different ways. The analytics take into account those Tweeps (Twitter users) who have over 1000 followers and can be viewed according to their general popularity (number of followers), their popularity amongst their peers (taking into consideration how many other philosophers follow that particular philosopher), or by women. There are 379 individual philosophers on Twitter, 100 of which are women (as at April 21, 2017). Note that the number of female philosophers on Twitter accurately reflects that only approximately 24% of employed academic philosophers are women (furthermore, women only made up 30% of all philosophy degree completions in 2009 in America – see APA online for more statistics). The Philosophy Organizations list on Twitter requires a minimum of 500 followers to be included, and that list boasts 115 users (as at April 21, 2017).

In this way, philosophers may use Twitter to network, to add (limited) commentary to public issues or to share links into the Twittersphere. Importantly, though, it is a public space in which anyone can access the ideas of philosophers with a Twitter Handle, and journalists can reach out to academics for ideas and interview opportunities. The space is dynamic and reciprocal in that, similarly, those using Twitter can pitch ideas or try to gain attention for a cause, a published piece of their writing or share their own interviews and the like with a broader audience. Academics can also self-publish via websites, blogs, podcasts and the like, again finding ways of making their ideas or the ideas of famous philosophers or classical philosophical thought experiments accessible to the general public. There are some philosophy magazines aimed at a general audience for which philosophers write, including *Philosophy Now*, which was launched in England in 1991 and is edited by Rick Lewis, and the more recent Australian publication *New Philosopher*. Many philosophers who engage in this way in the public media space are endeavouring to stimulate excitement about ideas, generate interesting conversations and stir up enthusiasm for the study of philosophy itself. Such public philosophers are also often working to assist individuals to engage critically and ethically with issues that pertain to our everyday lives. Happily, this public engagement is once again starting to be recognised and valued even within the academy, as evidenced by the statement released on 18 May 2017 by the American Philosophical Association board of officers in support of philosophers' participation in the public arena (http://blog.apaonline.org/2017/05/18/apa-statement-on-valuing-public-philosophy/).

It may be that those members of the general public who are engaging with the work and ideas of philosophers via outlets other than peer-reviewed academic sources are already critically engaged citizens. Yet this does not dismiss the important role of public intellectuals, even in the overcrowded Web 2.0 media space, to offer critical commentary and insights into contemporary debates and issues that affect the general populace. If anything, the need for more public debate that is both critical *and* compassionate may be seen as a call to arms for philosophers to engage more in the public sphere, and to do so with displays of *compassion*, as opposed to being solely analytically critical. Trained philosophers are ideally suited to help clarify and critique arguments that occur within the public setting, by focussing attention on to the ethically relevant features of such debates and highlighting pertinent facts that relate to the issues under discussion. The ideal of a democratic society works well only if its constituents are educated enough to be able to vote for the most reasonable policies and put people into positions of power who will be able to provide leadership for the common good, rather than serving egoistic goals. Thus any contributions to public debate that may elevate the level of dialogue and encourage a critically perspectival engagement with what is said, done or reported upon is a welcome and necessary addition to our society.

In highlighting the importance of critical perspectivism in today's society, I also illuminate a role for the philosopher as public intellectual. Without detracting from the important work done by philosophers within the academy, philosophers also have a role to play in public spaces, including online forums. As an expert with relevant thinking skills, the inclusion of philosophers in public debates would benefit society provided they demonstrate a critically perspectival attitude. The role of the philosopher as public intellectual may be a different role from the philosophically minded facilitator of a philosophy café who has the relevant skills to facilitate a well-functioning CoI. Either way, philosophers can (ideally) serve as role models for good thinking skills and add a critical and yet compassionate voice to issues of importance under public scrutiny and debate.

Critically perspectival citizens

Our technology continues to evolve and is increasingly immediate, globally connected and similar to face-to-face engagement; for instance, consider how accessible it now is to play an augmented reality game on a mobile device, hold an international business meeting across multiple locations or stay in touch with friends and family all over the world in various time zones. It is not at all unrealistic to think that online CoIs may be successfully facilitated with participants from all over the world. Without being restricted by physical location, it would be interesting to conduct empirical studies on whether the virtual CoI is as effective as the face-to-face CoI in supporting the practise of critical perspectivism.

If the online CoI is utilised effectively, this opens up further possibilities for educational innovations including student activities, teacher training and other forms of professional development, support and mentoring. It is my hope that technology and media may be used in innovative, positive ways to allow those who may lack the requisite support and mentors in their hometown to join an online community of like-minded others.

How will critically perspectival citizens engage with the technology of the future? While there is no set answer to this question, and rightly so given the creative manifestations of technology and the human imagination are unpredictable, by adopting the attitude of critical perspectivism, individuals will be able to engage with multiple perspectives in a critical, yet compassionate manner. The ethical attention imbued in the critically perspectival approach is of vital significance if the future use of technology is to be creative, socially minded, politically and environmentally responsible, as opposed to destructive and self-serving (or solely economically driven). It is critical, creative, and socially minded individuals that are required to guide public policy and societal flourishing in our technologically charged world, and these individuals are also the employees most desired by prospective employers.

There is a desire for future employees to be good problem solvers, to be critical and creative as well as good at working with others. In 2016 the World Economic Forum released a list of the top 10 skills for 2020 and these are listed below:

* Complex problem solving
* Critical thinking
* Creativity
* People management
* Coordinating with others
* Emotional intelligence
* Judgement and decision-making

- Service orientation
- Negotiation
- Cognitive flexibility

Collard (2016) notes that it is surprising how few employers or students feel as though young people are being trained to have such skills. Part of the difficulty educational institutions face is that we cannot predict the jobs that our future society will need, or even if we can predict them, we struggle to imagine how new technologies will alter these roles. For example, if we train a primary school–aged student how to use a computer today, this skill set is going to be redundant by the time that person is out in the workplace because of how quickly the technology is changing as new inventions are rapidly altering the way we use technology in our everyday lives. The solutions of the future will not be things we can even conceive of today. This explains why there is a global movement in education to refer to abilities and capabilities because these will be what future citizens require: transferable skills. Skills such as adaptability, work ethic and a moral compass that encourages us to treat each others as valuable members of a community are always going to be important and useful and thus worthy of cultivation.

This account of humans as artistic, creative, and as great innovators points to our curiosity. These attributes ensure that humans continue to explore ideas and seek new ways of representing our world, engaging with our environment, and communicating with one another. In understanding human nature in this way, we can see that we are not doing anything unnatural or radically different when we explore technological means of mediating our lived experiences. Rather, we will continue to explore various ways of representing our ideas and sharing our experiences with one another, and we will continue to exploit technology for these purposes. Therefore, the important issue at stake for educators is that of providing young people with the opportunity to learn useful cognitive and affective skills that can assist them when they use technology and engage with social media platforms. If adults can similarly be taught to engage critically, creatively and compassionately with multimedia and Web 2.0, this will result in more people adopting the attitude of critical perspectivism, particularly online.

The intellectual and affective skills that employers seek are also the skills that are useful in everyday life as we make moral (and other) decisions and judge information for credibility and reliability. These same skills are involved in adopting an attitude of critical perspectivism. Furthermore, it has been argued that these same skills may be cultivated within the P4C classroom, particularly being practised within CoIs. They are transferable skills that help us to live well, to flourish, and to make wise decisions about what we should do and why, even if we cannot perfectly predict future trends and innovations. Society needs critical thinkers who are also engaged morally as citizens, people who are compassionate as well as practical. If we can educate the citizens of the future to be critically perspectival, they will have the skills required to be able to work together collaboratively in order to discover, create and implement solutions to issues such as climate change and its effects, poverty and displaced persons, increased globalisation, rampant consumerism and other ramifications of the neoliberal agenda.

Global citizens

By adopting an attitude of critical perspectivism, we may come to think of ourselves as global citizens. The global citizen is someone who recognises others as more similar than different to oneself, even while taking seriously individual, social, cultural and political differences between people. Global citizens come together and unite in the recognition that we should all care about planet earth and that all people have a shared interest in living well. In a pragmatic sense, global citizens will support policies that extend aid beyond national borders and cultivate respectful and reciprocal relationships with others regardless of geographical distance. Peter Singer (2002), Martha Nussbaum (2012), and Naomi Klein (2010; 2014) have all argued in support of the notion of the global citizen.

Defending the idea of "one world", Peter Singer claims:

> A global ethic should not stop at, or give great significance to, national boundaries. National sovereignty has no *intrinsic* moral weight. What weight national sovereignty does have comes from the role that an international principle requiring respect for national sovereignty plays, in normal circumstances, in promoting peaceful relationships between states.
>
> (Singer, 2002, pp. 163–164)

He goes on to argue that "we should be developing the ethical foundations of the coming era of a single world community" (Singer, 2002, p. 216). He also acknowledges that this establishment of a single world community "is a daunting moral and intellectual challenge, but one we cannot refuse to take up. The future of the world depends on how well we meet it" (Singer, 2002, p. 219).

Similarly, Nussbaum notes the difficulty democratic approaches to politics will face given the diversity of people and ways of life, particularly taking into account religious diversity (2012, p. 240). She argues that consistency is not everything we need. "We also need correct and informed moral perceptions, in order to make sure that our arguments are not self-serving. And we've also suggested that these attitudes of curiosity, empathy, and friendship help to sustain commitments to good principles that might fray in times of stress" (Nussbaum, 2012, pp. 320–321).

The global citizen sees others as friends, and again the notion of caring and not just critical engagement with others is highlighted on Nussbaum's account. She reminds us that the imagination (our capacity for creativity) helps to cultivate our 'inner eyes' which are required to truly understand that others are vulnerable to suffering in much the same way that we are, a recognition acknowledged by the global citizen. As detailed in chapter two, here the role for compassionate concern in our treatment of others becomes apparent:

> Empathy is just one ingredient in a moral argument. Putting yourself in the place of another does not tell you whether they are right or fair: only linking their view of the world to an overall ethical argument will do that. Empathy, however, does do something important, showing us the human reality of other people whom we might have seen as disgusting or subhuman, or as mere aliens and threats.
>
> (Nussbaum, 2012, p. 231)

Nussbaum claims that empathy must be directed towards others we do not know as well as towards those to whom we are partial; namely, it must be an inclusive moral attitude if it is to function well. The global citizen cares about others, while also being critically engaged with the social, political and ethical issues of their world. Caring about others we do not know, have never met, and who may seem very different to ourselves can be a challenge, particularly at times when there is a climate of fear. Nussbaum characterises our contemporary world as fearful – particularly fearful, anxious, and suspicious of religious diversity, as debates surrounding the extremist actions of a minority of religiously motivated terrorists will attest, along with any other number of racist policies, such as calls to ban the burqa. In such fearful times, Nussbaum highlights the importance of cultivating our 'inner eyes' and being able to "see the world from the perspective of minority experience" (2012, p. 59) as a way of overcoming fear and intolerance.

As the current form of globalisation is cloaked in the garb of consumerism, Naomi Klein considers the positive effects that could emerge from this trend. "With globalisation, there needs to be some common standards" (2010, p. 439), she claims. The backlash against the corporate brand culture could well hold powerful multinational companies to account in an era that seeks transparency even as it is seduced by advertising. Klein notes,

> By attempting to enclose our shared culture in sanitized and controlled brand cocoons, these corporations have themselves created the surge of opposition . . . By abandoning their traditional role as direct, secure employers to pursue their branding dreams, they have lost the loyalty that once protected them from citizen rage.
>
> (2010, p. 441)

The manifestation of the neoliberal agenda in terms of consumerism may make room for the global citizen:

> The claustrophobic sense of despair that has so often accompanied the colonization of public space and the loss of secure work begins to lift when one starts to think about the possibilities for a truly globally minded society, one

that would include not just economics and capital, but global citizens, global rights and global responsibilities as well.

(Klein, 2010, p. 442)

Resistance to globally branded consumerism may indeed take the form of globally minded citizens who, for instance, care about the others who produce goods for their consumption at a lower cost of production. This opposition often finds expression via the Internet and social media platforms to espouse and further their causes. This can be powerful and effective, as evident with the 'we are the 99%' campaign launched by the Occupy movement in the USA, which quickly gained worldwide recognition and momentum. The campaign was launched following criticism of economic inequality in which 'the 1%' refers to the top 1% of wealthiest people in America who have a disproportionate share of capital and political influence. The majority (the 99%) recognise that their labours and taxes support the 1% given the nature of official governmental and banking policies that favour the wealthy, ensuring that the rich get richer and the gap between rich and poor widens. The global citizen is angered by such injustice; they seek equality.

The global citizen necessarily adopts the attitude of critical perspectivism. They critically assess various points of view, arguments and assumptions in search of truth and wisdom. They make use of the Internet and Web 2.0 to further their understanding as well as their causes. They care about others who live all over the world, in a variety of circumstances and with a diversity of religious and political beliefs. The global citizen desires a world that is shared, sustainable, and that supports peaceful coexistence – although they know that this is not an easy thing to achieve.

Conclusion

As technology changes rapidly, we cannot predict what future technological trends or social media platforms will look like. We can guess that there will be more augmented reality games, robots, and artificial intelligence (AI), but there will also be many other unexpected innovations that will transform the way we do things. What we do know is that if we concentrate on educating citizens to be critically and ethically engaged with the new innovations and technology created, we stand a better chance of using these inventions for the betterment of what is increasingly a global society.

The best approach for educators to take is to educate citizens to be critical, creative, compassionate and able to work with others collaboratively both online and face-to-face. Educational institutions need to catch up and keep up with the speed of individual technological literacy. New technologies and Web 2.0 are redefining basic notions of what it means to be literate and the importance of multiliteracies is now apparent. Children today are learning more about literacy outside of school than in classrooms, particularly through electronic and digital devices and software. Educational institutions cannot afford to ignore these new media platforms and teachers need to look critically at the influence of media on literacies that are formed as much outside as they are within the classroom. Technological tools must be embraced as literacy is reinventing itself, yet the critical thinking skills required to engage with such tools remain the same and can thus be taught within the classroom or in public spaces. While critical thinking and compassionate engagement with others can be cultivated within educative spaces, particular attention should be paid to how critical thinking and caring responses should be applied to engagement with online media and social media.

While it may be difficult to predict the effect our social media use may have in the future, it is important that those using such media are encouraged to do so critically and with care for others with whom they engage or to whom they refer. This pertains to the information users of social media pass along, the images they share, like and post, and other microcontent they believe, add to, and disseminate. Teaching people to be critically yet compassionately engaged global citizens who are able to effectively negotiate multiple perspectives is a necessary skill in our technologically infused world. Using philosophy as a praxis highlights the important role philosophers may take in educational as well as public spaces. Cognitive skills and affective skills such as those required by critically perspectival citizens may be taught through the study of philosophy and practised within a community of inquiry. CoIs may be facilitated in schools and classrooms, or in public spaces such as philosophy cafés. Taking philosophy beyond the academy is more important now in the post-truth era than ever previously and philosophers ought to engage in public debates in such a way that adds clarity to the arguments being espoused while also demonstrating relevant moral nuance to the issues under discussion.

Throughout this book, I have argued that people should adopt a moral attitude I have called critical perspectivism. Critical perspectivism is a manner of being appropriately critical and caring towards others with whom one engages both online as well as face-to-face and to information and images received from multimedia sources. I have argued that one way to educate people to be critically discerning as well as ethically engaged global citizens is by teaching them philosophical thinking skills and practising such transferable thinking skills as members of a community of inquiry. In this way, the study and, importantly, practise of philosophy can help students cultivate an attitude of critical perspectivism, particularly when a community of inquiry focusses upon a provocation or stimulus pertaining to Web 2.0 and smart technology. Philosophical thinking skills will support the attitude of critical perspectivism, and it is the cultivation of this attitude that will result in ethically motivated, globally minded citizens.

References

APA online: The website for the American Philosophical Association. Retrieved April 22, 2017, from www.apaonline.org/?page=data

Collard, P. (2016). *Creativity, culture and education: The international foundation for creative learning.* Retrieved October 2, 2016, from www.creativitycultureeducation. org/paul-collard

Greene, M., & Griffiths, M. (2008). Feminism, philosophy and education: Imagining public spaces. In N. Blake, P. Smeyers, R. D. Smith, & P. Standish (Eds.), *The Blackwell guide to the philosophy of education*. Oxford: John Wiley & Sons.

Herman, D. (2017, January 31). Whatever happened to the public intellectual? *New Statesman*. Retrieved April 22, 2017, from www.newstatesman.com/culture/books/2017/01/whatever-happened-public-intellectual

Klein, N. (2010). *No logo*. New York: Picador.

Klein, N. (2014). *This changes everything: Capitalism vs. the climate*. New York: Simon & Schuster.

Levmore, S., & Nussbaum, M. C. (Eds.). (2010). *The offensive Internet: Speech, privacy and reputation*. Cambridge: Harvard University Press.

Nussbaum, M. C. (2012). *The new religious intolerance: Overcoming the politics of fear in an anxious age*. Cambridge: The Belknap Press of Harvard University Press.

Randell, M. (2004). Constructing participation spaces. *Community Development Journal, 39*(2), 144–155.

Singer, P. (2002). *One world: The ethics of globalisation*. Melbourne: Text Publishing Company.

World Economic Forum. (2016). *The 10 skills you need to thrive in the fourth industrial revolution*. Written by Gray, A. Retrieved October 22, 2016, from www.weforum.org/agenda/2016/01/the-10-skills-you-need-to-thrive-in-the-fourth-industrial-revolution/

Index

Understanding Media: The Extensions of Man 78
urban legends 83
Usher, R. 79–80

virtual public sphere 11–13, 91
virtue ethics 5, 20, 22–23, 25–26, 30, 36, 40, 50
virtue/s 2, 12–14, 19, 22–23, 26, 28, 32, 35, 40, 48, 50, 79, 87, 93, 103, 106
Vygotsky, Lev 96

Warnock, Mary 113
Wartenberg, Thomas 6, 55, 56, 62–64
Web 2.0 3, 11, 31; critical perspectivism applied to 104–105; extended mind hypothesis of 78; "golden rule"

and 79; multiliteracies and 76–77; participatory mode of engagement and 80; as powerful political tool 80–82; public intellectuals and 113–114; public philosophy and 110–112; universal language of 79; *see also* social media
Weil, Simone 25, 42
Weitz, M. 59–60
Wilde, Oscar 45
Williams, Bernard 28, 113
Winstanley, Carrie 10, 95
wisdom 101, 113
work-at-home scam 84
World Economic Forum 115–116

Young, J. O. 44
YouTube 76